DISTANCES

DISTANCES

A PERSONAL EVOCATION OF PEOPLE AND PLACES

Stewart Conn

SCOTTISH CULTURAL PRESS

First published 2001 by

SCOTTISH CULTURAL PRESS

Unit 13d, Newbattle Abbey Business Annexe
Newbattle Road, DALKEITH EH22 3LJ Scotland
Tel: +44 (0)131 660 6366 • Fax: +44 (0)131 660 6414
Email: info@scottishbooks.com
website: www.scottishbooks.com

BRITISH LIBRARY CATALOGUING IN PUBLICATION DATA
A catalogue record for this book is available from the British Library

ISBN: 1 84017 043 3

Printed and bound by Bell & Bain Ltd, Glasgow

for Judy,
Arthur and Ian

OTHER BOOKS BY STEWART CONN

Poetry

Stolen Light: Selected Poems (Bloodaxe)
At the Aviary (Snailpress)
In the Blood (Bloodaxe)
The Luncheon of the Boating Party (Bloodaxe)
In the Kibble Palace (Bloodaxe)
Under the Ice (Hutchinson)
An Ear to the Ground (Hutchinson)
Stoats in the Sunlight (Hutchinson)
Thunder in the Air (Akros)

Plays

'The Burning' in *Scots Plays of the Seventies* (Scottish Cultural Press)
'Play Donkey' in *A Decade's Drama* (Woodhouse Books)
Thistlewood (Woodhouse Books)
The Aquarium and Other Plays (John Calder)
'The King' in *Penguin New English Dramatists, 14*
'Fancy Seeing You, Then' in *Playbill Two* (Hutchinson)

Also

co-editor of *The Ice Horses* (Scottish Cultural Press)
co-editor of *Scottish Short Stories* (Collins)
editor of *PEN New Poems* (Hutchinson)

BIOGRAPHICAL NOTE

Stewart Conn was born in Glasgow in 1936 and grew up in Kilmarnock. He now lives in Edinburgh. His recent dramatic works include a version of George Mackay Brown's *Greenvoe*, set to music for the St Magnus Festival, and *Clay Bull*, premiered by the Edinburgh Royal Lyceum Company and then broadcast.

His poetry collections have won awards from the Scottish Arts Council and the Society of Authors, among others, while *An Ear to the Ground* was a Poetry Book Society Choice. His latest volume, *Stolen Light: Selected Poems*, was short-listed for the Saltire Prize.

ACKNOWLEDGEMENTS

The author and publisher thank the following for permission to republish those essays which have previously seen the light of day, though not necessarily in their present form: **The Scotsman** (*The Rim of Hell, Horn of Sorrow* and *The Family Final*); **The Herald** (*Barcelona Fantasies*); **The Scottish Review** (*Remembered Skies, Malcolm's Land, Zev, Darkness into Light* and *Blossom Time*); **Chapman** (*Two Summers*), **Friends and Kangaroos/New Writing Scotland 17** (*M. Bouzou*), **Scottish Book Collector** (*Dead Letters*), **Scottish Field** (*An Ayrshire Boyhood*), **scrutiny2** (*The Heart in Exile*) and **Southfields** (*From the Wilderness*). Acknowledgements are also made to **The Listener** and to **Scotland on Sunday**.

Thanks are due to the editors of these publications in which a number of the poems have appeared or are due to appear: **L'ànima del teixidor** (Edicions Proa, Barcelona), **Back to the Light** (Mariscat Press/Glasgow City Council), **Dragoncards** (Mandeville Press), **Edinburgh & the Borders in Verse** (Secker & Warburg), **The Dark Horse, The London Magazine, Poetry Scotland** and **The Scots Magazine**.

Thanks are expressed to those writers and copyright-holders who gave permission for quotations from published work: most sources are indicated within the essays. Specific acknowledgements are: for extracts from *Selected Poems 1954–83, Following a Lark* and *For the Islands I Sing* by George Mackay Brown to John Murray (Publishers) Ltd; from W. S. Graham's *Collected Poems 1942–1977* (Faber and Faber Ltd) to the Estate of W.S. Graham; from *From the Wilderness* by Alasdair Maclean (Victor Gollancz Ltd) to the Alasdair Maclean Estate; from *Collected Poems* and *The Leaf and the Marble* by Iain Crichton Smith to Carcanet Press Ltd; from *The Well at the World's End* by Neil M. Gunn (Faber and Faber Ltd) to Dairmid Gunn; and from Allan Spence's *Stone Garden and Other Stories* (Phoenix House) to the author.

Grateful acknowledgements are due to Donalda Smith for permission to draw on unpublished letters from Iain Crichton Smith; to Ellen Craig and the Edward Gordon Craig, C. H. Estate for an unpublished inscription and note by Edward Gordon Craig; to Neville Dubow (ed.) and the Irma Stern Estate for extracts from *Paradise: the Journal and Letters of Irma Stern* (Chameleon Press); and to Christopher Whyte for an extract (on Pompeu Fabra) from his translation of a study of Catalan by Josep Murgades (Chapman 88/Window on Catalonia).

The author warmly thanks Archie and Elizabeth Bevan, Gunnie Moberg, Gus Ferguson, Ian and Meta Gilmour, Pauline MacDonald, Joan Lingard, Michael and Margaret Snow, Ann and Julian Poole, Gerry Cambridge, Donny O'Rourke, Ros Taylor, Sue Meek and Shaun Belcher through all of whom distances were bridged. A deep indebtedness is expressed to Brian Pugh and Avril Gray of Scottish Cultural Press, through whose encouragement and belief this volume has come to fruition.

CONTENTS

An Ayrshire Boyhood

My parents moved to Kilmarnock when I was five. Early on my father was told by another clergyman that St Marnock's, the town-centre charge to which he'd gone, 'wasn't on the map': in other words it was working rather than middle class based. At one extreme were London Road, its surgeons' sons packed off to boarding-school; Dundonald Road's comfy villas extending west; and further afield the mansions and mini-chateaux of the Rowallans and their ilk. At the other were the cramped slums of Fore Street, behind the cross and overdue for demolition; housing schemes like Onthank; and beyond, rows of deteriorating cottages like those still known as Peace and Plenty.

The bus station was even then a bottleneck. It would get worse later, with traffic crawling to the coast. The railway station was seedy and gaslit, its pedestrian tunnel dank and leaking, laughably at odds with the monocled Johnnie Walker stepping it out on shiny posters: 'born 1820, still going strong'. On a manual turntable, the Infirmary as a backdrop, great steam-locomotives revolved slowly. The cobbles down to John Finnie Street were lined with metal cart-runners for the dray-horses. The town extended from Beansburn past the camouflaged cooling-towers to Riccarton parish in the south. Despite its carpet and other industries, its engineering works and distillery, the air was unpolluted and clean to breathe.

The dominant atmosphere was one of cosy congregationalism. Half an hour away was Ayr, Athens to Kilmarnock's Sparta. The county town, it had its avenues and green swards, its racecourse and frivolous theatre. That was where we'd head eventually, on Saturdays: in the morning, to the Ice-Rink; in the evening to the County Hotel, then the Pavilion to listen to Harry Margolis and his band – and hope to chat up those of the bonnie lasses who hadn't gone to the Bobby Jones in search of American airmen.

Our grey stone manse was draughty. But it had a big back garden with kennels, a hedge cut in the shape of a peacock, and a small pond. On my first visit I peered through six inches of ice at the goldfishes, blurred below. They survived that winter, but a gull got them in the end. For the remainder of the war part of the lawn served as a chicken-coop. Later there were ducks, but my mother put her foot down at the threat of a pig. One by one our cats were lured away by neighbours, only to be run over and returned for burial.

The boy next door played the clarinet and his record collection introduced me to the Hot Five, Jelly Roll Morton and Muggsy Spannier. Together we scoured Caprington Estate for chestnuts, which we bored and heated in the oven, then varnished to play at conkers. Sore knuckles time.

Our garden was great for cricket. If the ball hit a branch before bouncing, you were caught. Broken branches, especially those bearing fruit or blossom, had to be dumped over the wall. Into the fish-pond was six and out. For real cricket there was Kirkstyle, with its creaky sight-screens and shacky little pavilion. The Rev. James Aitchison, one of Scotland's most elegant batsmen, was at his stylish peak and a gleaming miner called Matt Colquhoun kept shattering the stumps at the bing end. All year round it was football, in the playground or on the cinder pitches in the Howard Park. After one game my first real leather football rolled under an A1 bus: the biggest bang I'd ever heard. In winter we skated on New Farm Loch or went sledging: one year this was stopped abruptly, and fatally, when one of our classmates careered off the slope and into a barbed-wire fence.

I loathed the rugby-only Academy with its squat tower. I'd come through the primary school in the old fee-paying days of penny loaves, when maroon caps floated down the Marnock Water like outsize rowan-berries. The Infants Mistress Annie C. McLarty, F.E.I.S., a formidable figure to us, was highly regarded as an educationist. Our qualifying teacher Davy Gordon retired in 1953 after 36 years at the school. A subsequent Academy history says, with dry understatement, that he 'will be remembered by many former pupils as a strict disciplinarian who wore, among other items of clothing, starched collars and a bowler hat every day to school except once a year on Sports Day when a cloth cap replaced the bowler'. He also wore green-tinted spectacles. To him justice was an exquisite instrument. Once when a boy wouldn't own up to talking in class he gave us all 500 lines. At the interval everyone streamed out and chased the culprit to the lavvies. Back in class we sat cross-armed while the snottery figure was brought out to the floor and leathered. Then Davy turned: 'Rest of the class another 500 lines. For bullying'.

In senior school the classicists were an elite. Fifth and sixth years were geared to the bursary comp. After I'd left, the head of the French Department behaved as if bereaved because a favoured pupil (not me) only got a third at Aberdeen. Our extramural education was in the town's cafes and cinemas: the plush upholstery of the Plaza or the Empire's double-seats preferable to the George or the Salon, the local fleapit – but costlier. For some there were the snooker saloons. For others the Dick Institute library and museum. Happy hours were spent browsing among its shelves or keeping assignations beside the draped butterfly cases. Night closing in and the rain rippling down the windows, it was like being inside an aquarium.

There, not at school, I first came across poets who were still alive, some actually Scottish: through *Lines* and the *Saltire Review*, the William Maclellan imprints, books by W.S. Graham, Ruthven Todd and Adam Drinan. At a broad polished table in the reading-room I scribbled my first putative poems, then hammered them out at home on my father's heavy-duty Underwood. At eighteen I fell for Dylan Thomas's *Collected Poems*. Though there were (and remain) quite a few I couldn't make head nor tail of, they were great to declaim in the bath. Their euphonious pantheism, Freudianisms and verbal bravura took some dislodging from the system. Almost as big an encumbrance was the polo-necked pullover I deferentially wore in all weathers.

Sundays were an ordeal: the long walk down the aisle to the manse pew is embedded in my memory. I can visualise the interior of St Marnock's, light slanting across the communion-table, the font with its flowers. The tree in the vestibule, and carols, at Christmas. Sheaves of corn round the red sand-stone pillars, for Harvest Festival. The Sunday school trooping out before the collection was, in that nice Presbyterian term, uplifted. Or a choir member having to tap our blind organist on the shoulder when he launched into a verse too many – and his extravagant final fortissimo, to make it seem intentional.

And my father: black robe, red and purple hood; arm raised in benediction. I remember him, without sentimentality, as one of the most stimulating preachers I've heard: reducing theology to brass tacks. Not that I'd have dreamt of admitting that to him – if I was even aware of it – at the time. His children's addresses were something else. Once he produced a white mouse, which promptly vanished up his sleeve. Another time he broke and swallowed a raw egg, by way of some spiritual analogy – although also, I suspect, to shock my mother.

But what made me really squirm was when he began, 'A small boy of my acquaintance . . . '. I felt so conspicuous, sitting with my sisters in the manse pew, gazed down on (so I imagined – I'm sure they never gave me as much as a thought) by the ranks of Killie worthies in the gallery opposite. Beyond that an overwhelming sense of St Marnock's and all in it, miniscule under the gaze of an all-seeing and all-hearing God. One woman parishioner left a legacy for nothing so banal as the dry-rot fund, but a carillon of bells. There was no guarantee the tower would be strong enough to hold them. Little doubt, to whose glory the gift was really intended.

Within the past few years the stonework, tower and roof have again undergone extensive renovation; the church interior having itself been redecorated. The carillon has not only been preserved, but is apparently 'ranked 12th in the United Kingdom'. And the *Ayrshire and Arran Architectural Guide* speaks of the building's 'wealth of Gothic Revival decoration from the battlemented tower and the hood-moulded door, to inside, the pulpit, an expression of the crescendo of Gothic Revival'. Not something that impressed itself on us then.

Many of my father's views were enlightened for the times. Ecumenically for instance: among his friends were priests from nearby Coodham retreat. Once a visiting Jesuit stayed in the manse. And another time Toyohiko Kagawa, a missionary from Japan. He let us see (but not touch) model rickshaws and houses; then prayed alone in the study, before preaching to a packed church. My father also believed unmarried mothers should be helped, not spurned as 'fallen women': the prevailing view in those days on the Kirk's committees. No wonder he made a habit of getting up the *Kilmarnock Standard*'s nose.

The notion of Christians as 'standard-bearers' was part and parcel of his thinking. He deplored social or 'Sunday only' members; and those on the roll who attended only twice a year – but were the most demanding when it came to matches, hatches and dispatches. He never tried to force me to join Church. I never did. On Billy Graham's first visit to the Kelvin Hall,

I yearned desperately (if a mite over-passively) to be struck by the light. But another part of me found the manipulation, and mass hysteria, repellent. And I've a hunch that whatever Hereafter my father may inhabit, whether beyond the orbit of the Starship Enterprise or deep in my own heart, he'd be the first to sense if I were to enrol for the wrong reasons.

Golf courses stretch like a green patchwork down Ayrshire's coastline. You could strike a golf-ball continuously, from one end to the other. Unless you lost it, that is. On summer holidays in Troon I'd be on the municipal links from dawn till dusk. You could play with another holiday-maker – or on your own. Except you were never really alone: in your fantasies you'd alternate as one or other of your idols. My most dramatic moment wasn't a hole in one but (I must have been big-hitter Roberto de Vicenzo at the time) a hooked drive that bounced on the main road then hit a double-decker bus.

My father joined Barassie for the exercise and not, like so many, for the 19th. In 1947 Dai Rees won a Daily Mail Tournament there: walking down the last fairway, a hand on my shoulder, he said I'd been his good-luck mascot. His prize must have been all of £250. A year later a Scot called Reid lost the British Boys' Final to a J.D. Pritchett. On the trudge back to the clubhouse I got both autographs, then asked poor Reid if he'd mind adding 'runner-up'. Somehow he refrained from wrapping his niblick round my neck.

In my autograph book are the dour Henry Cotton, Fred Daly, Norman von Nida (86 as I write, and advising Nick Faldo on his grip) and Bobby Locke. Locke's Open win at Troon is a painful memory. A group of us plunked school for it. An evening paper had a photo of us round one green. Next morning we were called to the rector's study, and belted. As fashions changed we'd try out assorted hats, wind-cheaters, two-tone shoes with frilly tongues. My father scorned sartorial extravagance. Mercifully he discarded his dog-collar. And his old waterproof jacket wasn't so bad. But in rain he'd put on bicycle-clips, so that his turn-ups wouldn't get bedraggled. This made me all the more desperate to beat him. I never did.

My first clubs had hickory shafts, the irons needing sand-papered to keep the rust off. My favourite wood – a lady's club I suspect, as it didn't have to be sawn down – was called a brassie-cleek: one day the head rocketed into the rough, loops of thread unravelling behind it. Envious of more muscular schoolmates I hammered a piece of lead-pipe to an old driver, to broaden my shoulders and add length off the tee: all it did was give my swing a loop that ruined it for life. Our home courses were Caprington and later, soggy Annanhill.

I recall one other happy activity. While still at school I'd joined the Kilmarnock Amateur Dramatic Society. We performed in S.C.D.A. competitions and Festivals. Little visiting drama came our way, though. Whether as the Palace or the Exchange, the local theatre had a history of being dark or boarded up – and at least once abandoned to bingo. Resident companies would bite the dust. When I left to do National Service, I shared a compartment in the train south with a mournful director and three tearful and now out-of-work actresses. In their luggage, I remember, was a well-shaken bowl of goldfishes.

Once I'd done my square-bashing I was posted to RAF Swinderby. There wasn't much to do in the flatlands of Lincolnshire other than cross-country running – and joining the station drama club. Which I did. The one production I was in was Agatha Christie's 'Murder at the Vicarage'. The only male member who was non-commissioned, I was cast as the murderer. My return two years later was to a very different Kilmarnock – and family situation. Soon after, I left for good.

Kilmarnock, a Burgh of Barony since 1591 and with its coat-of-arms (double motto: *Confido* and *Virtute et Industria*) supported by squirrels, had long been a trading centre. In the early 19th century it grew in importance with the Industrial Revolution. Its weavers and bonnet-makers flourished. Coal had to be got to the coast. A planned canal didn't materialise but in 1812 the Kilmarnock & Troon Railway, the first in Scotland built under Parliamentary authority, opened. Andrew Barclay (locomotive builders) and Glenfield & Kennedy (hydraulic engineers) established worldwide reputations. Gregory, Thomson & Company began carpet manufacturing. Among household names during my schooldays were Massey-Ferguson (tractors, combines and other farm machinery), Saxone (shoes), B.M.K. and Glacier Metal.

The economic decline of the 1970s would change things, not only in Kilmarnock but for the lace-making towns up the valley which could no longer compete with cheap imports. Pit closures led devastatingly, as the '80s progressed, to even greater unemployment. And despite attempts to attract light industry and fresh investment the whole area (like the Borders, their mill towns the latest victims) remains economically depressed. This my school generation, and our parents, were fortunate to be spared. We were aware of pockets of poverty, and I remember my father's concern for parishioners who were starting to be laid off. But on nothing like the scale seen since.

Again too, perspectives and attitudes were different then. The grown-ups were able to look back on the War (many on two Wars) and food rationing; or on the Depression with its soup-kitchens, its lassitude and despair. Nor did we dream how polarised society would become, or of the complacency of a Government under which avarice and self-interest would be not merely tolerated but nurtured. In that sense our lives were privileged. To us though, they merely passed. Most satisfyingly for me, not even in Kilmarnock but outside its boundaries.

Three miles to the south, looking across to Ailsa Craig and Arran's Sleeping Warrior, was one of Ayrshire's many dairy farms. On my father's side of the family ownership and before that the tenancy of this farm, Harelaw, went back beyond Burns's day. If I felt I belonged anywhere it was on those tilled and tilting acres; in the knowes with their lime-pits where a horse and cart were said to have plunged and disappeared; on those pastures and quarry-slopes.

Saturdays and breaks were spent on the farm. There was the shed where the ferrets were caged and I fought the billy-goat, his skull like iron. There were sick heifers struggling to their feet as soon as the vet slid the byre-door open. Each ne'erday the farmers held a shoot, combing the quarry slopes for rabbits and hares, the spoils divided and hung up to drip, as they settled before a roaring fire. I was once held upside-down at the big mill, having handfuls of chaff stuffed up my trouser-legs. At the milking one of my father's aunts would handle the queys, moving slowly in her clogs and apron, dipping a finger in the froth to keep the teats moist. Next morning the cans went to Riccarton creamery, where the milk was tested and poured into a great vat.

Those were the days of oil-lamps, and sounds in the dark. As I lay in bed, I'd tug the covers up to keep out the scrabblings. One image stays with me. Two Polish prisoners worked on the farm for a while. One day as I arrived on my bike, I saw them at the entrance to the stackyard. I couldn't make out what was going on. Until I saw a prancing shape, then something rising and falling. They were killing a couple of goats, with a heavy hammer.

There was hay-time and riding to the stack-yard on the bouncing ruck-lifter. The spreading of lime and sowing of seed, from the traditional canvas tray strapped round the neck. There were midges and clegs. Rats scrabbling in the straw. Above all there was my father's Uncle Todd. Tall, white and bony, he seemed an almost mythic figure: a cross between the White Knight and an Old Testament prophet. He once sacked a landgirl for whistling on the sabbath. One day he pinned me with his stick to the whitewashed byre-foot, took out a wad of paper and started declaiming slowly and throatily. After what seemed an age he stopped.

'Well, who do you think wrote that?'

'Robbie Burns, Uncle?'

'Not a bit of it. It was masel'.'

There was a twinkle in his watery blue eyes. I had given the reply he wanted. It turned out this was a ritual everyone in the family underwent, at one time or another. Each time, he got the same answer. Once though he was stopped in his tracks (or tracts). On being introduced to my mother, he wasted no time: 'Tell me lass, are you saved?' Looking him in the eye she replied stiffly, 'I'm a member of the Presbyterian Church of Scotland'. He didn't broach religion with her again.

It was on the farm, not at school, that Robert Burns first impinged on me. He was spoken of (albeit within strict confines: the extent of his fornicatory activities, and The Merry Muses, were later revelations) as naturally as if he was part of an extended family. In class we recited 'To a Mouse' and 'My Luve is like a Red, Red Rose' and had to listen to various teachers' renditions of 'Tam o' Shanter'. But it is in Todd's throaty voice that I hear:

> *The rank is but the guinea's stamp,*
> *The man's the gowd, for a' that . . .*

I assumed that over the years, through my own accent and peppering of Scots, I had retained at least a residual trace of my Ayrshire upbringing. Until back years later for a writers' workshop, I was forcefully told: 'You're no frae Killie, you're bliddy English!', so mim-mou'd had I evidently become: one penalty perhaps, of supping ower-lang with the BBC. More recently I'd a reminder of Burns's immediacy – against his being, as so often elsewhere, regarded as a remote figure on a plinth, to be dusted down annually. I'd been invited to Irvine Burns Club. When I was introduced as from Edinburgh, there were looks of dismay – and instant retribution:

'Edinburgh! Wi' its snobberies and soirees. It damnt near destroyed him!' There was the sense that he might have left the room, a moment before.

At Kilmarnock Academy in my day Scots was tolerated in Burns, but clamped down on otherwise. The poems and songs were approved as art-objects; but to be severed in our minds and mouths from any wider social or cultural context. That's to say, we had to learn them (paradoxically 'by *heart*') while virtually disavowing the tradition they sprang from. No such dichotomy on the farm. There the poems registered on my ear as a patterned extension of common speech, not as elocution exercises. And Todd's own fire-and-brimstone verses were in the tongue he customarily spoke:

> *O wha shall be able to staun*
> *Prepared for the great Bridal feast,*
> *Only they wha obey the command*
> *And escape the mark o the beast.*

> *It will come like the crack o a gun*
> *And the door for ever clink ta,*
> *Few, few shall hear the well done*
> *And the many be left ta their wae.*

Todd's grandfather had the reputation of being the strongest man in Ayrshire: he could take up a pair of cart-wheels by the axle and walk away with them. His son John Cochrane worked Harelaw under three landlords and five factors. He died in 1913, the oldest farmer in Craigie parish. The year before, he'd taken his turn at the ploughing. And he was a fine horseman. His twelve children had included Todd and Hugh. For a while it had been Hugh's job to take the stallion round the farms. One day it bolted. Hugh had a foot crushed – in his twenties and lamed for life.

Another time my father (himself a boy) was with Hugh and Todd in a gig. Halfway down Craigie Hill the pony took fright at something, and away it went. All three finished up in the hedge. The pony was finally found on the main Ayr road. Some years later the same thing happened. My vision of Ayrshire was of runaway ponies and figures shooting headlong over hedges, like something from a Charlie Chaplin film.

All his days Todd bred and traded horses: he'd travel miles on foot to buy an old rickle of bones anyone else would have had put down. To nurse them he'd spend nights in the stable, putting on blankets, heating tar, applying nauseous poultices and mixing patent cures. He'd then sell them on to the Co-Op. By the end of the War either Ayrshire had run out of old nags, or the Co-Op had more than they could cope with: either way, the bottom fell out of the market.

To him, anything new-fangled was of the Devil: the electric milking machine, or the new Fordson tractor. He and his stooped sisters were of a narrow religious sect. When my father was staying and studying for the ministry, all three burst in and announced that they'd received the Gift of Utterance from the Holy Ghost. The world was due to end at noon the following Tuesday: would he climb Craigie Hill with them, to pray. He refused. They succeeded, on their own, in keeping the last trump at bay. Twice a week, on the Sabbath and for the mart, Todd would dress in style: stubble trimmed, butterfly-collar stiff, gold watch-chain showing. In the front room stood silver cups from his trotting days. On the wall was a tinted print from some mansion-house sale showing a shiny black mare, the American Girl, 'winning from Miss Lucy Palmer and Lady Thorn at Naragansett Park, Providence in June 1869'. With this went hissing oil lamps, the ticking of the grandfather clock, the fluttering of moths and the purring of muscovy cats.

Not long after Todd died the farm went out of the family for good. His hearse should have been horse-drawn. But times and fashions change. So does landscape. Kilmarnock's housing schemes increasingly encroached, with their tins and litter. On a first visit after the farm had been sold I peered through a pall at new outbuildings, razed huts and strange contours. The knowes had been filled in, the land flattened. Trucks and bulldozers worked by a smouldering dump. The quarry was overgrown, fence-posts rotted, its honeysuckle bedraggled. Myxomatosis had come in the interim, and swollen-headed rabbits hobbled across the track or cowered by the verge. It seemed part of an inevitable, implacable process.

Not long ago, back at the Academy for the first time since leaving school, I met the friendly young headmistress who is the latest successor to the aloof *ore rotundo* mandarin of my day. In the sunny new library batches of Higher English pupils were alert and fresh-faced, prefects still sporting maroon blazers with yellow cording, and the badge with its scrolled *Do Justly, Love Mercy, Walk Humbly*. After our sessions came a tour of the Old Building, with the librarian and a member of the English Department. Where I'd had Latin conjugations bullied and belted into me an animated German lesson was in progress. Rooms hummed with computers. From the tower roof we saw a sparrow-hawk swoop and disappear. On the undulating skyline what remained of Craigie Hill and its gouged-out quarry were scarcely discernible.

In the intervening years these farmlands had come to be identified with my youth, also remote and irretrievable. Where I'd had access I was now a trespasser, an interloper. Yet to this day I retain an enduring sense of possession, albeit through dispossession. A way of life may have slipped away – the necessary price of progress: one on which I was never economically dependent, and my links with which it would be silly to exaggerate or sentimentalise. For all that, no matter how mythologised my memories have become or how fanciful they may have been in the first place, they remain related to real people – a sturdy breed who belonged to a specific soil, as it belonged (for a while) to them.

The Family Final

During World War Two scrap-iron was melted down to make bombs or bombers, I wasn't quite sure which. Garden-railings were sawn off and carted away. But not in our street. Some said this was because we were in line between the mart and the slaughter-house. We knew better: it was to keep the visiting orange and green hordes at bay. We were three minutes from Rugby Park. When I was small I'd peer through our net curtains at the crowds.

As soon as my school-pals and I started going to home games, we'd have to wait for a grown-up to lift us over the turnstile, then scamper behind the near goal. For the Wee Team, the corrugated-iron gates were opened at half-time and we'd get in free. Later we had 'our' crush-barrier facing the stand. In 1947 when I was ten, Killie were relegated for the first time. The next year new manager Alex Hastings' son was briefly in my class. One Friday after school we were playing three-and-in on the sacred turf after it had been cut and sanded. We got a thick ear and I was banned for two home games. For a while we were friendly with a local undertaker's son: there was quite a to-do when we were discovered playing wee heidies in his yard, upright coffins for goals.

Around then my father played in a charity match for the Ministers against the Toon Cooncillors. He tore down the wing like a Presbyterian Jinky Johnstone as I shouted 'Come on, wee Conn!' – taking care he didn't know it was me. Those of us from the town thought we were the bees' knees: sophisticates compared to others from the rural areas or up the valley. The wind was fair taken out of our sails by a throaty Clyde fan's 'Get intae thae coun'ry yo-kels.'

Hugh Taylor's Club History records that Dundee beat Killie in the '52–53 League Cup Final. Then promotion. But four years on I was doing National Service in Lincolnshire, when the Bairns won *that* replay. 'No worst, there is none' said Manley Hopkins. A lot he knew. From 1960–62: runners-up in the League, plus *three* cup finals lost. Two to Rangers, the last to Hearts. After one, insult was added to injury: late on in the Dark Horse Restaurant, the team found there was a free bar no one had bothered telling them about.

Richard, one of my friends at the time, wasn't just a rabid fan: his father was three-times chairman of the directors. Through him we got to all the away games. For the atmosphere we preferred the terracing to the stand. But we were once ejected from the Ibrox directors' box for booing big Don Kichenbrand, and asking what stone they'd found him under, after he'd appeared to spit in Willie Toner's face.

As for those cup finals it wasn't the defeats, or even things like Frank Beattie's memorably chalked-off goal, that stuck in the craw. But the journeys back across Fenwick Moor, like a series of corteges. To be met by pathetic huddles of wee boys waving bedraggled flags. Losing to Rangers was always worst. I remember sitting outside the dressing-room as then trainer Walter McCrae chatted to Willie Waddell. 'I hate going to Ibrox,' said McCrae. 'If they beat you, it's never a defeat. They make it a *humiliation.*'

By the time of the last-gasp .04-of-a-goal League win over Hearts I was married and away from Ayrshire. Richard had been in a bad car crash at the Fenwick road-end. He lay for months in the Victoria. When he regained consciousness, he'd lost his memory. One day in desperation, I took in my blue and white striped scarf and bunnet, and draped them at his bed-head. Soon he was trying to smile, or grimace, at what they conjured up. When he came out, I hadn't the heart to ask for them back. Anyway, they'd served their purpose.

Over the decades, we lost touch. Before the Big Saturday I wondered if he'd be there. And what it would be like. In the event, it was glorious. And in many ways, touching. In the mutual respect of the managers – and Alex Totten's decency. The fans' intensity, yet sporting harmony. The 'family final' the press rather patronisingly called it. Meaning 'provincial'. But this was in the best sense true. Of the communities, and their support. In the Broomloan Stand we rubbed shoulders with lads and lasses who'll remember the occasion as I will, to their dying day. With somewhere in the crush the Clan McIlvanney. And at the final whistle a whirling delirium and the added spice of booing wee Farry the S.F.A. secretary who had issued a killjoy dossier, to put the tin lid on any celebrations.

I don't know when I last saw a football game and wasn't sickened by obscene chants and sectarianism, and undercurrents the media turn a blind eye to. Any sporadic sparks on Saturday (I saw just one, and that in the city centre) showed no signs of igniting further. The cup won and lost, both sets of supporters applauded *both* teams. Outside Ibrox after, there was congratulation and commiseration. No whiff of threat or triumphalism. Even back at Central Station, in my new scarf, I was approached by dejected Falkirk fans offering handshakes and saying well done. I sympathised. 'Could only be one winner' was the reply. Maybe. But at times, it was a bit close for comfort . . .

I've written in a poem that despite my years away

I still think of my shoes
holding a sprinkling of rich Ayrshire soil.

At times I'd wonder if this was just a literary conceit, maybe even a shade fraudulent. But the wet eyes at the final whistle suggest a lingering something, which has resisted cultural blandishment and survived geographical disenfranchisement.

This sense of belonging stems partly from place and partly through an awareness of blood-links, of residual family ties. Does this extend to my own sons? No way. Nor is there any reason why it should. Both were brought up in the east. For them, there was no thread to be severed: Ayrshire merely an alien half-moon on a map. As a Dundee United supporter during their spell as serial runners-up, the older boy tholed his own (maybe even worse) assize. But his real passion has been for cricket; while the younger's formative wounds were received on the rugby field.

As for me, last Saturday couldn't have been more satisfyingly worth the wait. Whether for a year, another 40 years – or another lifetime – who knows? And who cares? All that matters is the compensatory silver-ware of the here and now. So all thoughts of Europe to one side for the present. Hats off, to Bobby Williamson and the boys! Let them savour it. Only next time, can someone please send me the words of 'Paper Roses'?

> P.S. Too late: this slushy old Marie Osmond song was replaced the following year by an adapted version of 'The Halls of Montezuma', the hymn of the U.S. Marines.

Remembered Skies

The *Scottish Field* had asked for a piece on 'the Ayrshire of my boyhood'. I did it and thought no more about it. Then they said would I go with one of their Pic-men, for an illustration. Town or country didn't matter: so long as it caught what I'd called 'those *inimitable skies* . . . so clear over the years'. I met the Pic-man and we made for his car. Then we headed south. No one had allowed for the rain. It began just after Newton Mearns. By the time we reached Kilmarnock it was coming down in buckets.

'You'd think it was the Fair – how's about a bite and see if it clears?' said the Pic-man.

We had a pie and a pint in the Wee Thack. Still a steady drizzle.

'Time we were offski,' said the Pic-man.

'Any point?'

'I'll not get any mileage if I don't go back with some pics.'

As we parked the sky opened like a sluice. The farm seemed smaller than before. And somehow naked. The knowes had been filled in. There wasn't a tree left. The Pic-man sat morosely. Then he stubbed his fag, zipped up his anorak, grabbed his camera and clambered out. I followed up the mushy slope overlooking the farm. This made it look even barer. Beyond was a municipal dump, steaming gently like a huge cow-pat. The sky was like ash. His camera clicked, in the gloom. On the way back, we crossed the Fenwick Moor in silence. Nearing Glasgow:

'Want dropped off?'

'Bridge Street'll do. I can get the underground. Sorry about the weather.'

'Not your fault.'

'Who wrote the bloody piece?'

'Cheer up.'

'Why?'

'Never heard of the Bandy Hope?'

The next month the magazine came out. I opened it. The photo was perfect: a spacious sky, the bunched cumulus fleecy and unmarred by rain. I rang the Pic-man.

'About that photograph – '

'Not inimitable enough?'

'It's *magic*. How'd you do it?'

'No problem. The sky being all uniform. Soon as I got the negs I went up to the Pic-library. Found "*Autumn Scene, Perthshire*". Simply cut it on.'

READING MATTER

The Glasgow Herald, *delivered on week-days,*
read avidly for its front-page obituaries
and financial news. Saturday's
Standard *gave the cattle-mart prices.*

Both would end up wrapping cheese pieces
carried out to the fields in wicker baskets
by great-aunts wearing frayed straw hats,
as gravely as though they bore the loaves and fishes.

All that was permitted on Sundays, the Bible.
But each month a splash of colour –
National Geographic, *its yellow cover*
garish against the patterned wallpaper.

And the People's Friend *once a week*
to be pored over in private
then reappear torn into squares, stuck
on a metal hook in the outside toilet.

The Rim of Hell

ARRIVAL (APRIL 1984)

First port of call: Rivonia, in Sandton suburb. On the fringe of Johannesburg. An opulence such as I've never known. Round the house where I'm a paying guest, azure-necked peacocks strut. The pool, lit from below. Trellises with vine. Lemon and pomegranate trees. Ibis screeching. Incessant barking of dogs. Smack in the mink and manure belt; in its post-Raj way, more English than the English. Now that I'm here, almost impossible to accept I'm in the South Africa of my preconceptions and premonitions. Variously, for the notebook:

> *There's been a drought for so long, the plants are all shrivelled.*
> *We have to keep the pool topped up, for fear it cracks . . .*
> *Look, there are blacks everywhere. Apartheid just doesn't exist any more.*
> *We hardly even knew about the Soweto riots. I mean, the foreign press exaggerates everything.*

A drive to Pretoria with its forbidding prison, ostentatious State Theatre, and rows of fern-like jacaranda trees. The grounds of Melrose House where the treaty of 1902 was signed – and I imagine Kitchener's rigid figure ringed by pretty officers with butterfly nets cavorting on the lawn. On the way there and back, blacks at bus-stops, in what shade they could find. Brightly clothed, like scatterings of confetti. Otherwise they scarcely impinge.

I'm wakened in the morning by feet pattering outside my bedroom door. Then a screech. Not the peacocks. 'Get yourself together, girl. Where is the newspaper, hey? And why haven't you damn well cleaned the master's shoes?' In an adjunct to the main house two blonde girls, expensively clothed and perfumed: their job, to collect and 'look after' racing drivers here for the Grand Prix. Each morning, I'm taken in the Alfa-Romeo to an underground city car park. My host takes the lift to his office. I do my own thing, join him again for the journey back. Before the week is out, I lose the stomach for it. Trapped in a luxurious cocoon, I decide to move on. At the end of the last day I lean from the car window to shake hands with the uniformed attendant. 'Go well,' he says. The engine revs impatiently.

JOHANNESBURG

I tramp this ruthless sulphurous metropolis. Bounded by bleak highway, the massive gold-mine deposits of its origin on its periphery, like sores. Sophiatown-born Mongane Wally Serote's

> *Jo'burg City, you are dry like death,*
> *Jo'burg City, Johannesburg, Jo'burg City.*

> – 'CITY JOHANNESBURG' –

This is from *Yakhal'Inkomo* which means 'the cry of cattle at the slaughterhouse'. It pairs powerfully with another paperback I've just bought: Oswald Mtshali's *Sounds of a Cowhide Drum*.

Next, Hillbrow tower. The big multi-nationals: Shell, Nestlé, the rest. John Vorster building, with its infamous tenth floor. At intersections, Mercedes saloons and buses the colour of avocado, crammed with black workers, their faces expressionless. Pasty whites scurrying, on foot. City of contrasts. Joubert Park, with its fountains and pigeons, where I sit and read. The Art Gallery: outside, a chess game in progress, using huge pieces. Noord Straat, with its perpetual throngs and *niet blankes* toilets. The milling railway station. Curio shops with grotesque masks. The trendy

Market Theatre complex; on its walls, posters for plays by names whose London agent claimed not long ago that she'd make sure none of *her* writers would break the cultural boycott. At night, a ghost town. The migrant labourers having been taken back to Soweto. The whites to their suburbs, each with its plush shopping mall, trees and fountains under cover of glass.

It's really spooky, so it is. There's nobody there. Just black faces.

Heading for the theatre we swerve to avoid a black youth prancing in the roadway, another after him with a knife. As we pass, he is into him. They rock together as though caught in an irresistable slipstream.

This city has knife-wounds like other places have influenza.

The play is *Inyang Ema*: Black Dog. At one point an actor threateningly grips a heavy chain then swings it round his head, to create a helicopter: the most striking image of the evening. In the early hours, in the tiny brick 'cottage' where I sleep, I lie restlessly. Crickets chirrup like demented alarm-clocks. In the distance, the interminable rumble of these frightful trains, transporting their human freight.

At the end of the next week I drive by way of Ladysmith and sprawling Pietermaritzburg, to call on Alan Paton. To deliver a cassette copy of *Too Late the Phalarope*, my dramatisation of which he'd approved; and to shake his hand on behalf of a borstal governor friend in Edinburgh, as a gesture of respect for Paton's rehabilitation work as principal of Diepkloof Reformatory. Through the Valley of a Thousand Hills, all aloes and misty vistas . . . to Hillcrest.

Paton over eighty. White-haired, eyes alert, with a philosophic breadth of mind and conversation. His study stacked with books. In his typewriter an opening sentence – *'This is the second and I hope final volume of my autobiography'* – with 'and I hope final' scored through. His talk of Glasgow, where his father was from; of conscience; and of the land he loves, then in a state of emergency. As I drive away, night falling, his frail figure waves goodbye. And thrumming through my mind, a phrase from the novel, and a first precept whether at Diepkloof or in the wider world: 'To punish and not to restore, that is the greatest of all offences.'

DURBAN

City of irreconcilables. The sea-front, with its floodlit hotels. Raucous funfares and garish arcades. Cafes packed with holiday-makers: a whole stratum absent in Johannesburg. And a strikingly different racial mix. Durban has half a million Indians: more than any city outside India. Lunch in a tasteful Chinese restaurant (the Chinese classed, as are the Japanese, as 'honorary whites') with Pat Poovalingham, formerly of the President's Council, now leader of the Solidarity party competing for seats in the Indian chamber of the tripartite council. He has strong views on segmental autonomy. He thinks there will be an eventual fourth chamber, 'not right away, in three or four years maybe'. He is prepared to work towards this. Give it a chance.

The founders of the United Democratic Party, among them Helen Joseph and Dr Alan Boesak, see things differently. A Government treading water: blacks permanently excluded. The previous month I'd spoken briefly to Boesak in Edinburgh where he was delivering a series of lectures. He came across as a hypnotic power-player in a dog-collar, with fine-honed gestures and seductive cadences. (Subsequent evidence of, it seems, greed and money-siphoning would bring a prison sentence and disgrace: a sad nemesis for a man who had spoken out so boldly and articulately during the struggle.)

Indelible images of Durban: bathers beside notices reserving the best stretches of beach, and children's playpools, for 'the sole use of the White Race Group'; and in the attractive Botanic Gardens, a khaki-clad warden striding 200 yards to stop a lovely Indian girl and her boyfriend embracing on the lawn – then retreating to sit once more, like a mantis in the shade.

I'd started off in a grubby hotel near the sea-front: the only time I've slept with a chair-back under the door-handle. But the only intruders were the armies of cockroaches clacking down a ventilator shaft at my window. After two sleepless nights, I hand in my room-key and toilet-roll, and move to a pleasing Victorian hotel near the Botanics. Each morning the Indian head waiter deferentially keeps me up to date with things. He expresses so keen an interest in poetry that when I leave I give him, as well as a tip, a signed copy of one of my books. As I approach the main swing-doors, the remainder of the dining-room staff are lined up, awaiting theirs. I flee.

I set off on the return drive to Johannesburg by way of Inanda township. Decorated mud-huts. Beautiful women wearing a flat Zulu headgear, rich red like a nimbus, on which they bear heavy water-pots.

When I raise my camera they shield their faces. I follow a wide arc, through Swaziland. To be waved down by a line of flak-jacketed soldiers with rifles. The customs search is thorough; even my portable typewriter held upside-down and shaken. In that evening's *Citizen*: a report of a search for four ANC escapees, recaptured after a gun battle.

CAPE TOWN

As I fasten my seat-belt for departure from Jan Smuts a stetsoned Texan starts talking. He is still going on volubly as we approach Cape Town, about racism: not here but in America's Deep South. Table Mountain lives up to expectation. Then the nubble of Signal Hill. Beyond, the Atlantic and the blur of Robben Island, on which the English Service last night announced in mellifluous tones the release of an undisclosed number of penguins. Odd to think the first person to use the island as a convict settlement was Jamie the Saxt: but only after he became James I of England.

Each morning, the taped wail of the muezzin, from the Malay quarter across from my hotel window. One evening, to the city hall for Mahler's first symphony: a grand bout of timpandemonium. Visits to the outlying Baxter Theatre. First the premiere of *Skeyf*, on white liberal angst and the pressures of military service. Then a packed and hysterical house for *Total Onslaught*, a one-man show by satirist-impersonator Pieter-Dirk Uys. I found it all the more disconcerting, with its sense of collusion between the well-heeled exclusively white audience who are the targets of some of his sharpest barbs, and the performer in his role of licensed court jester.

Inland through wine country, to stately Stellenbosch. Exquisite buildings with spacious Dutch interiors and honey-coloured furniture. The University, breeding-ground of political Afrikanerdom – both line-toeing and renegade. In Cape Town itself and the suburb of Rondebosch, guilt is almost tangible among those I meet. And an urging (almost a pleading) that I stay long enough to see the wonders of the Cape and understand 'how we can bear to live here'. In *Bateleur Poets* (the imprint taking its name from the short-tailed African eagle) I find a selection 'Thresholds of Tolerance' by Lionel Abrahams. Johannesburg's unofficial laureate, he nurtured and promoted the work of Serote and Mtshali. Here he takes a different pulse:

Two cars, three loos, a swimming pool,
Investment paintings, kids at a private school . . .
we entertain with shows or gourmet food —
and yet we don't feel right, we don't feel good . . .

we've got those lost-man, late-man,
money-man, superman,
whiteman blues . . .

– 'The Whiteman Blues' –

Back to the dust and desolation that was District Six. Only a church and a mosque have survived the bulldozers. Despite being a prime site close to the city centre, it remains undeveloped – a lasting symbol of injustice. Poet Sue Clark takes me to the brutalised township of Langa to meet her playwright friend Fatima Dike – who has lived there all her life and says she loves it. Then to Crossroads, squatters in their tens of thousands living in tin excrescences. With pallisades of stick, it is like the remnant of a mediaeval city. Even more heartrending, the KTC camp, a mini-town whose pathetic structures, mainly of wattle branches and plastic bags, have to be hidden each morning before the police come with dogs to tear them down.

Before leaving Cape Town I meet Jeremy Cronin. While he was serving a seven-year sentence for distributing illegal pamphlets, his wife died of a brain tumour. Her mother was allowed to visit him, by special dispensation, for 15 minutes. Between them a glass plate, preventing either from comforting the other. Cronin writes movingly and with lyrical elegance, of his prison experience, in a recent collection of poems *Inside*. It implicitly advocates vigilance, so that attempts can be made to at least restrain the torturer.

From the plane when I left could be seen another scar on the landscape. Khayelitsha, destined if the Government has its way, to become home for a quarter of a million blacks, removed by force from Langa, Nyanga and other townships. These would then form a coloured buffer-community, strengthening the Cape's labour market policy. Oblivious to human suffering, one cabinet minister remarked of Khayelitsha, 'It has one of the best sea views in the Cape Peninsula.'

ON THE MOVE

Twice during the latter part of my two-month stay I felt impelled to leave South African soil. One journey took me by way of the irrigated grainlands of Western Transvaal, then the scrub and red earth of Bophuthatswana, to Botswana. Passing through Mafeking en route: the main road a churn of mud from the first rain in two years. In Gaborone I was all but deafened by Hugh Masekela's over-amplified flugelhorn; and any hopes I had of taping exiled poet Keorapetsi Kgositsile (a professor in the University there with whom I had enjoyed an animated and for me instructive conversation) foundered on Black Consciousness mistrust, and an awareness that any recordings I made would have to pass through South Africa.

Back in Cape Town, I'd been courteously invited with Sue Clark to dine at the home of theatre producer Moyra Fine. The guests included Van Zyl Slabbert, leader of the Progressive Party: polished, articulate and persuasive in his views and aims for a better South Africa. But in Gaborone any notion of his party being an 'Opposition' in any other than the most naive sense, is mocked. So too, as patronising and ineffectual, is the definition of Helen Suzman as in any way 'the blacks' white hope'. Paton's outmoded liberalism is also a devalued currency – even among those who were his own. A new generation has been born. Everywhere, the barking of dogs. And the crowing of cocks, presaging a blood-red dawn . . .

I'd indulged in the notion of a last-minute trip to Zimbabwe, to see the Victoria Falls. On the way we fly over the Limpopo. The scale and majesty of the Falls releases that part of my mind which had been battened down. Out at five in the morning, I have the rainforest gloriously to myself before the coach parties arrive. And Australian back-packers, inevitably hallooing. Cataracts and chasms of light, spanned by rainbows. Rainforest and iridescent birds. Myself incongruous with umbrella and waterproof trousers, but naked torso drenched. I come to a shaky wooden notice right on the lip of the drop: just legible, 'Do not pass this point'.

I photograph the statue of Livingstone, arm outstretched. Then downstream, cross a narrow bridge, through clouds of blue butterflies, to set foot in Zambia. And stand on the edge of the mighty Zambesi. A fusion of tears and laughter, in trembling liberation. Subsequently zebra and giraffe in their natural habitat. Wildebeast grunting, throughout the humid night. A crocodile farm. Impala, bounding under a muslin moon. Then back to the hub.

SOWETO

I'd already glimpsed Alexandra. In the early morning, with the smoke from many fires suggesting that powdery semi-opaqueness I'd seen only in films. When the car slowed down, a group of men ran at the car. It turned out they were after work. My friend explained to them, in their language. They waved us on. We skirted the remnants of Sophiatown; passed through Orlando, dominated by a mighty power-station which serves Johannesburg. A section of Soweto is excited at the prospect of electricity: they've been waiting forty years and because they're on the national grid, will pay more.

My guide to Soweto is the Rev. Bernard Spong, humane director of the Interchurch Media Programme. Through him I gain an insight into the work of the South African Council of Churches who have rejected violence as a means of overthrowing authority – as well as institutionalised violence, such as detention without trial. Increasingly though, it has come to express the legitimate aspirations of the black people. And it does not consider a non-violent Church as necessarily passive, or pacifist.

Its general secretary Bishop Desmond Tutu is constantly under scrutiny. The SAAC's activities are minutely scrutinised in the recently released 451-page Eloff Report. Its real value is as a compendium of Tutu's statements and principles. In one typical speech he called for common citizenship, the abolition of the pass laws and a stop to population removals. Prime Minister P.W. Botha's response amounted to little more than a claim that apartheid had been 'misunderstood' throughout the world: 'I am not prepared to lead [my People] on the road to majority government on a one-man, one-vote system . . . That is not possible.'

All the more disturbing is that Botha's approach is considered dangerously liberal by the breakaway Afrikaner Volkswag; their televised founding meeting grotesque and repulsive with its crypto-Nazi uniforms, a crooked three-legged cross, and chillingly imitative salutes.

I shall not forget the faces of Soweto's unemployed, the rows of nameless streets, desolate among their detritus; the single men's hostels, with their bitter implications; the wastelands never turned into the play-areas they were intended for; the riven faces of the elderly, runelled as by drought, among the ramshackle huts and outside latrines of Cliptown. The impact sharpened if anything, by the smiles we received; the life-force in evidence amidst desolation and deprivation. Bernard had in June 1976 seen the bodies of the massacred school-children, bullet wounds in their backs. We paused outside the stadium they'd been heading for, and gazed at the open space where shortly, on the anniversary, the police will again congregate with their clubs and shields, canisters of tear-gas at the ready.

In so far as the purpose of my visit to South Africa was to *see,* I suspect I saw, in the time at my disposal, about as much as I could bear. The shock-waves even now take me unawares. Among abiding impressions, the individual kindness and generosity of everyone I met, and with whom I stayed. And a degree of separateness beyond anything I'd been prepared for.

Outside a United Congregation pre-school nursery we are visiting, twenty chanting children are being taught the words for different colours in a language not their own. When they get over the novelty of my presence I take my pictures and saunter self-consciously to the street. A van screeches by, men in balaclavas dangling from it. They leap off, empty bins, are on and away. A coalman reins up, wets his eyebrows and poses as if to say, 'Take me'.

Later I'll scarcely recognise the photos of the more derelict areas. The squalid browns, even the brick latrines, seem picturesque in a way that rather than retaining their power to shock, defuses the rage that should augment pity. What, I ask Bernard, does one do? He gives me a look: '*The little one can.*' South Africa is a land of stunning diversity and boundless beauty. Exhilarating and thought-provoking. It is also, in the Dante-esque intricacy of its insidiously interlocking circles, as close to the rim of hell as I ever wish to be.

Horn of Sorrow

Morning in the bush; the air already an oven. Cries of lourie and hornbill. Kudu and zebra graze. The Pilanesberg National Park in Bophuthatswana. Suddenly the sounds are closer, more menacing: gibber of vervet monkeys, roar of rhino. But no need to run for the nearest tree. Look left, you'll see a green tarpaulin stretched against the glare. Beneath it, gyrating figures: Theatre For Africa's new group of actors rehearsing and improvising – in the heart of the environment that is the source of their work and which they so wish to see conserved.

Founded in 1989 by Nicholas Ellenbogen and his wife Liz Szymczak the Company have travelled as far afield as Hong Kong, Singapore, Switzerland, Germany and the States – and to several Edinburgh Festivals, winning *Scotsman* Fringe First and *Herald* Angel awards.

All of which could scarcely be more remote. This is Bophuthatswana's largest park, opened in 1979 by President Lucas Mangope. The game introduction programme 'Operation Genesis', also the largest of its kind, has involved the translocation of some 6,000 animals from all over southern Africa. The unique geology of the region and its diversity of vegetation and habitats can support a wide spectrum of animals. About 50 species of larger mammals and over 350 species of birds currently inhabit the carefully protected reserve.

Think concentric circles. An outer ring of hills: the eroded remnants of what hundreds of millions of years ago was an active volcano. This lava rim screens the thornveld from the outside world. Within it, a stone circle. Within that our camp. On the site of one of the ancient lost Iron Age villages of the Swana. Tents, a cooking space. And at the centre, a ring of expended ash; the world's navel. Morning and night, all snake-fang; but kept smoored, by day.

In rehearsal is *Horn of Sorrow*, on the plight and destruction of the black rhino and the temptation to the under privileged people of Africa to make money illegally. The narrator, a gangling hook-beaked Cape vulture ('I'm an endangered species myself'), keeps a paternal eye on one female rhino from birth to her death at the hands of poachers. This demands total concentration and disciplined ensemble playing.

All the animals and the sounds and milieu of the bush are created by the troupe. Stunning mimicry, clowning and African music blend – often wittily and with the simplest props. A baby rhino's birth is suggested with a large transparent plastic bag as the placenta from which the struggling infant frees herself. Audience identification with the actors as animals is so total that the poachers' greed and their hauling of a strand of barbed-wire across the stage have a powerfully disjunctive impact. So does their shooting the baby rhino with darts, then manhandling it for transportation.

Even more daring theatrically: *Kwamanzi* (Zulu for *Place of Water*). With no dialogue, choreography and mime provide the narrative: from drought, to rain. Birds probe ticks from hippos. A three-person giraffe straddles its forelegs, to drink. A red lamp behind a tautened drum-skin is the rising sun; rice trickling into another, oncoming rain. Meanwhile Man the Hunter becomes Man the Destroyer. The play ends on a note of pain – and warning. The play's beauty and authenticity rest wholly in the hands of the actors – who have no escape from the scrutiny of the director:

> – *Don't rush it: land, then seize with the talons. I want the grandeur of the bird.*
> – *You're not enjoying the sunshine on your flanks. We must see this.*
> – *At the bottom of the pond [to a bullfrog] you go dead. You mustn't. I want to sense your feet in the mud.*

Movement is honed, timing perfected.

— A leopard would never bend its forepaw like that, when it's striking.
— Your concentration's gone. Your props were all over.
— If you find the bushmen funny, you're lost.
— Think hyena. And don't rush it. Focus!

The directions demanding but positive, encouraging. A break for a Diet-Coke, then back to work. Overhead a snake-eagle spirals in a thermal. The baboon-bowffs are real. Other cries are recognisably thespian:

— My shoulders are killing me, hey.
— I'm getting so desperate. My protein's essential.

Zimbabwean, English and Afrikaans accents mingle with Zulu and Swana. After dinner animal movements and birdsong are meticulously studied on video and sound-tapes, under the expert tutelage of zoologist Richard Emslie from Edinburgh, who is currently based here. The session over he adds to the colour of the bush by cycling off to football practice in a Dunfermline strip. Back to our tents. Listening to the sound of crickets. Every so often a spiralling mini-whirlwind sucks dust and leaves into the air. We hope it avoids the clearing, and the fire-space. Lest its crazy zigzag should turn our tamed beast to cavortings of fire.

Something wondrous at being out at night, looking up at unfamiliar constellations. And the Southern Cross. Every so often, a shooting star. A sense of time and space so vast, the mind can scarcely cope. Then back to practicalities: and heading out from the tent, shovel and torch in hand, without my legs being again ripped in the prickly scrub. Stifled laughter from one of the other tents. A flashlight goes on, then off. I find my way back, guided by Nicholas's snores – logged as one of the region's more impressive wildlife phenomena. In no time the canvas panels will revert to red, white and blue: a cubed drapeau; as in a box-kite, the spirit transported high over Africa.

All too soon the weeks have gone by. Our departure coincides with the release of two prides of lions into the Park. For the last few days a helicopter has been tilting and buzzing back and forwards overhead, trailing the existing animal herds, taking a count and noting their travel patterns. The lions will have electronic tags so that their movements can be followed and their kills charted. Already high new electric fences have been going up round our camp-site. Fittingly by way of farewell, at dusk on our last night, a bull-elephant appears briefly and silently at a water-hole, billowing and ghostly, as though bearing the spirits of his ancestors.

The opening venue for the play is, bizarrely, Sun City. Or rather, the adjoining Lost City. The performance space a fake-Aztek amphitheatre adjoining King Sol's ulcerous casino-oasis with its raucous music and tit-and-bum shows, its one-arm bandits and fruit-machines played ceaselessly by pasty faced husbands and wives from the Transvaal and beyond, their features faded, eyes dead. Flyers were distributed throughout the massive glass and chrome Leggo-style hotel complex. But its occupants have other things on their minds. Black and white intermingle. On the way to the open-air auditorium with scalloped steps and fibre-glass ruined pillars, we pass through a gateway manned by hefty security men. Overhead a great dragon opens its mouth, belches flame. The bush now far away.

Needless to say, the cast are on edge. Scarcely anyone turns up. The acting wavers – then succumbs nervously to indiscipline and the wrong kind of comedy. That essential *focus*, and the *spirit* of the piece lost. For the new members of the cast, a real baptism of fire. And exhaustion. Mercifully the week-end is soon over. I've taken my photos of bird-like strelitzia flowers and loping wart-hog on the fringes of the golf complex – its fairways and greens incongruous against the burnt umber of the fringes then the arid terrain beyond.

In no time it's back in the combi, props stored and roped for the swaying journey eastward through what was a Swana stronghold before becoming an Afrikaner fiefdom; then the motorway skirting Pretoria; and back to Johannesburg, Hillbrow tower on the skyline, then other bursts of light with between, ominous patches of dark. For the Company, back to the rigours of the rehearsal-room and morning-class and as ever against a tight deadline, a new play to build in to their repertoire for Geneva – and beyond. A further mountain of Diet-Cokes and Amstel-tins, ahead.

My African stay ended with three days in the Moremi Wildlife Reserve, part of Botswana's magical Okavango Delta: a paradise of papyrus and reeds, slumbering hippo and detours round mercifully inert crocs. Based in the westerly Jedibe Camp I was poled across the lagoon in a mokoro by a

Shona boy whose name-badge read 'Trust'. He could instantly identify birds still to me no more than specks on the skyline, and was familiar with their names not just in his own tongue but also in English and Latin: aristocratic ibis and egret, the suave saddlebill and nesting maribou storks like scrawny bundles of flotsam, their apparent hauteur ill becoming their role as scavengers. Overhead, a pair of osprey circling. Then bunched high on the shaded fork of an evergreen, the birder's dream: a Pels fishing-owl, nocturnal and rare, no more than a blotch of ginger and grey. I could just make it out. Trust grinned, gave me the thumbs-up.

Before five next morning I was collected to be taken fishing. Myself in the prow, an elderly Zimbabwean farmer in the stern. Our boat moored to the reeds at a river intersection, we were tugged into midstream by the current. Our guide for the day, Water Two, caught three tiger fish, the Zimbabwean and myself barbel and bream. At one point my line screamed out almost to the backing, then slackened, bitten through. More barbel. African fish-eagles, on a similar ploy. Shortly after sun-up the mozzies took over, and we beat a hasty retreat. Tiger next time.

Over lunch we were introduced to a blonde and lissom former Miss South Africa, visiting the camp as part of a promotional tour. She let me photograph her left foot in its elegant size 6 shoe alongside my catch (literally as a foot-rule) to indicate their size. Then more bird-watching. Carmen bee-eaters performing mid-air acrobatics, then settling on a branch to remove the sting before eating. The breathtaking radiance of the lilac-breasted rollers. Irascible hornbills extending head and neck upwards, to emit vertical streamers of sound. Perjink jacanas – nicknamed 'lily trotters' – stilting across the lily-pads. And extravagantly exquisite on the water, purple gallinules performing, almost faster than I could take in, *entrechat* upon *entrechat*.

In the company for dinner that evening was Daryl Balfour, a wildlife photographer who had survived being charged and trampled by an elephant in Kruger National Park where he and his wife Sharna were researching their latest book. For a while he somehow managed to cling to one of its legs and avoid being gored by the fearful tusks. On recovering consciousness he fired three shots, the agreed distress-signal. The trackers found him, severely wounded, with the sandy soil churned all round where he lay. Spoor suggested that the elephant had tried to kneel on him to deliver the *coup de grâce*. He'd had surgery and was now recuperating. He sounded eager to return to the project – and curious as to how the same elephant would react, next time it saw him and sensed his smell.

Dark came early. To bed. A fusillade of moths and other heavy-bodied insects hurtled themselves against the glass of the storm-lamp over the verandah. Inside, the mosquito-nets firmly in place. For a while a hippo kept padding and grunting. And long into the night I could hear from the neighbouring tent the elderly Zimbabwean wheezing and regaling his companion with details of Mugabe's renewed farm sequestrations.

On the flight back over the Kalahari from Maun to Gabarone, my brief stay already a jewel in the brain, I looked down from the tiny plane on Deception Valley, sand stretching as far as the eye could see, with bursts of vegetation the colour of bruises. Below, the pure waters of the Delta, rather than form a great estuary, peter out in a depth of sand so great even major earth-tremors leave no trace, but are absorbed before they reach the surface. A terrain *in extremis*; in which I imagine, mirage-like, a bushman and his wife awaiting the hyenas through whom they will join their ancestors.

We flew over the great buffalo-fence, raised to contain the cattle but against which migrating antelope, cut off from their drinking-places, have died in literally their hundreds of thousands. There is a recurring threat that the water itself will be piped for industrial use, or for export, thereby killing countless more.

Elsewhere the row rages over ivory-poaching and the theft of rhino-horn as an aphrodisiac. The burning of ivory-mountains certainly seems the wrong way to resolve things: better surely to flood the market with it, so that the price falls – and the poachers are put out of business. Meanwhile the animals' plight and Man's destruction of the environment are on the increase.

Theatre For Africa's achievement lies not just in the courage of their convictions and in making a conservationist statement palatable, but in the imaginative vigour with which their shows are conceived and evolved; and (at their best) in the cohesion and conviction of their performances. What could in lesser hands fail gets across in a way that is visually, aurally and spiritually stimulating. And intensely theatrical. Later as I headed for home, it struck me as both touching and fitting that the name of the baby rhino in *Horn of Sorrow* should be *e'Tembaletu* – 'our *hope*'.

[1993]

The Heart in Exile

*Searching I roamed the world – to arrive at the origin – at beauty
– at truth – away from the lies of everyday – and my longing was
burning hot – then the darkness opened up and I stood at the
source of the Beginning – Paradise*

– IRMA STERN'S JOURNAL –

In a shaded corner of the Cape Town suburb of Rosebank is a white house
called the Firs. This was for four decades the home of Irma Stern, one of
South Africa's most important pioneer artists, and has since 1971 (five
years after her death) been a museum administered for her estate by the
University of Cape Town. A cool cavern amidst fountains and foliage, its
interior is crammed with Stern's own work and artefacts she collected: from
African carvings and masks, and bronzes and scrolls from the Far East, to
more contemporary ceramics. The furniture, late 15th century European
onwards, includes a magnificent English refectory table round which when
she held court, she would have her celebrated dinner parties.

In Stern, opposing worlds merged in a very real sense. Born in the
Transvaal in 1894 of German-Jewish stock she received her early training

in Germany. Her background and cultural lodestars were those of Europe, a war-torn Continent she escaped from, to return to the fiery landscapes of Southern Africa. In the 1920s she travelled widely in this Paradise, her 'land of strong colours' which provided her inspiration and artistic impetus, and about which she wrote an intense illustrated journal discovered only after her death. Sadly this could not in itself guarantee personal happiness. Her early Cape Town exhibitions were treated with puzzlement and hostility by critics and public alike, even her family showing displeasure.

By the '30s, however, she had won recognition at home and after a period of further intense activity in the Congo, Central Africa and Zanzibar her late period took her – as painter and collector – to France, Spain and other European countries. In sketches and photographs she comes across as increasingly heavy-featured, in one late sketch by the art critic F.L. Alexander, gross. One self-portrait suggests that she was able to contemplate and record this unflatteringly, with at least a twinkling of humour.

The breakdown of a marriage to a husband chosen for her saw her again expressing a longing for the intellectual stimulus of Europe. Later and estranged she may have taken a lover. Certainly in the autumn of her life and in almost Chekhovian mood, she seems to have sensed regeneration; still searching for what she could retain of Europe, yet transmute into something African. Perhaps not surprisingly the quality of her African works was acclaimed in Europe long before it was recognised in her native land. It was only the year before her death that she was awarded the Medal of Honour of the South African Academy for Science and Art.

Paradoxically she also felt a need to go, as she put it, 'where there was no sign of Europe, no trace of civilisation – just Africa lying in the sun . . . the natives lovely and happy children, laughing and singing and dancing through life with a peculiar animal-like beauty which adds a touch of the tragic to the expression of their faces – the heaviness of an awaking race not yet freed from the soil'. This and her sensuous depiction of Swazi girls come across as not far short of unabashed paternalism, despite the social change around her.

In his commentary to a luxuriously illustrated edition of her *Journal and Letters* Neville Dubow observes:

> In her later years Irma would wax bitter about what she took
> to be 'degenerative' European influences on the 'natives'. In
> conversation with her one gained the distinct impression that

her concern was less for the welfare of detribalised peoples reduced to imitating European modes, than for the fact that such people provided her with less compelling subject matter.

This was spelt out apparently in a broadcast interview with Professor Dubow, towards the end of her life. Her view of her subjects as exotics shows her lumbered with her colonial heritage, 'sad and worn out' though Europe was to her. This has been an enduring legacy: as has the dilemma: for whom is Africa (and which Africa) 'home'? In landscape painting and portraiture, and the temperature of a painter's palette, the locale of a work is very likely to be self-evident; deducible without recourse to verbalising or research. There being no language barrier, no intermediary is needed between eye and canvas. Much more difficult as regards writing: to locate in South African poetry in English for instance, a precise fault-line between the European and the African.

Noel Brettell was born in Worcestershire in 1908 and read English at Birmingham University. Having taught in Rhodesia and England he married and returned to Rhodesia where he died in 1991. He has been described by Douglas Livingstone as an 'undoubted giant of poetry in South Africa'; and seen by others as a colonial incomer akin to Blunden and Housman. Despite his having 'acclimatised' to the topography of Africa, I doubt whether future generations will realistically identify with him as a precursor.

An African imprint is detectable in the work of Roy Campbell (1902–57) prior to his self-imposed exile. On the strength of this and his translations he remains one of the finest poets the Continent has produced. Even then his mode remained resolutely anglicised; as did that of William Plomer (1903–73) whose remarkable novel *Turbott Wolfe* was a landmark in both English and South African literature. Guy Butler (b.1918) was hailed in the '60s as a 'true' South African. But for all his muscularity, or the rich compression and originality of Sydney Clouts (1926–82), more is needed than a profusion of local place-names and iconography. Many of their successors remain locked in a double tradition: not surprising in that many were educated in Great Britain or have taught here.

Patrick Cullinan was born in Pretoria in 1932. From the age of fourteen he was educated in Europe, mainly (because he had no choice) in England.

Returning to South Africa at twenty-one, his dilemma was whether he was in fact a European or an African:

> I remember sitting in a cottage in the Eastern Transvaal, on the Escarpment, thinking it through one night. When I woke up in the morning, I didn't have to think of it any longer: I was an African, and I always would be. I had truly come home, as it were. I did not feel that I was a European, nor did I want to be. But that I have an enormous amount of Europe in my make-up is something that I would never want to deny.

Cullinan believes there is something distinctive in South African English and his poetry, persuasively of being *in* a place, corroborates this: in the cadences English-speaking South Africans use, and perhaps in a particular sense of disquiet. Not always marked but there. Scottish poetry in English has clear parallels. But though today's new poets are African and not European born, I detect no equivalent imprint to that which has given American poetry its sonority and identity; or the subtle shifts of register through which Derek Walcott's *Omeros* is so triumphantly Caribbean. The nub may be that in each instance there are 'home-grown' languages to draw on.

Characteristic of white South African writing in recent decades has been its sense of exile, both in those who left during the Struggle and in those who remained. As Christopher Hope, describing his first visit to his native land for twelve years, put it in *White Boy Running* (Secker and Warburg): 'The sense of exile that we as English-speaking South Africans felt in our own country is something that has never left me. We were a generation who went into exile before we even left home. Leaving does not increase the sense of loss; returning does not cure it.'

Concerned at how impervious both the general public and the intelligentsia were to poetry, Leon de Kock and Ian Tromp edited *The Heart in Exile* (Penguin) from 'the best poems published in English since Mandela's release; poems of potentially breathtaking impact . . . in which the heart conceives of its exile in, from or within the imaginative entity we call South Africa'. Restricted to the transition period 1990–95 this was generally felt not to meet the expectations of its title. A poem in de Kock's subsequent collection *Bloodsong* (Snailpress) perceptively sets proof-reading the anthology against the blossoming jacarandas outside. Finely-textured and multi-layered, the closing lines embrace irreconcilables:

I cannot trust such spectral beauty,
it is a seduction soon to suffocate

in its own nectar, as the bees know,
who feed on the sweet souring of the scent.

– 'PRETORIA: OCTOBER 1995' –

It is dangerous to assume all émigré literature must be driven by a political or emotional spirit in turmoil. At the same time unconscious factors cannot be discounted. Basil Du Toit was drawn to poetry at school in the Eastern Cape. By 1980 when his first book *Home Truths* (Carrefour) came out he had been in Scotland eight years. In that period 'home' wasn't really anywhere to him. But though he felt no desire to return to South Africa, publication instilled 'a sense of coming into the tradition of South African poets, being one of the community of writers'. That helped to orientate him towards Africa. His *Older Women* (Snailpress) is more rooted in not just South but Southern Africa. This is consistent with his view that rather than poets remaining 'South' African, they should have a wider awareness of the Continent: 'For many years they were not able to travel, for political reasons – but poets still tried to expand the sensibility of other parts of Africa. And we do tend to think of a Southern African literary system – those sets of nations forming a literary community.'

To reach the widest possible audience black poets from M. Pascal Gwala to Mongane Wally Serote employed not an indigenous tongue but English: paradoxically the language of the discredited imperial power, in which Nadine Gordimer wrote the novels which won her the Nobel Prize for Literature – and the lingua franca Afrikaans can never become. (Contrast the term 'American writing', which prior to the blossoming of writers who included Toni Morrison – another Nobel laureate – was virtually interchangeable with white, with 'African literature', so long synonymous with black.)

That there are so many books by white poets is largely thanks to the enterprise of small publishers such as Carrefour, David Phillip and Gus Ferguson's redoubtable Snailpress. But with too many poets and too few readers, bringing out a slim volume is like dropping a nail-clipping off Table Mountain – and awaiting the splash. The publishers' resources are so slender, they are constantly under threat. Of paramount importance are the preservation and extension of the traditions essential to any mixed culture's life-blood. But is what's needed now a recouping and re-channelling of resources and energy – and an allowing for the time this takes? With the overthrow of the apartheid regime old-style protest poetry, much of it in any case so politicised as to squeeze out the poetry, lost momentum or required redefinition: not only a new impulse is still being sought, but a new identity – and vision. Another by-product of prolonged internal exile can be an urge towards self-immolation. How can this in turn be healed and re-channelled? The answer is no easier within any art form than for the individual or the national psyche it mirrors.

In Cape Town in 1996 I saw an exhibition marking the Soweto uprising. The installations were uniformly angst-ridden, some horrific. So was much of the work by students and children I was shown. Is this part of an inevitable catharsis, a shedding of cumulative guilt or unburdening of anger? If so, will these artists change, or could it take generations to come to terms with the past – and exorcise its demons? For them as for the Society they mirror, they must come to terms with that past, before they can confront the future. This cannot evade a complex social and psychological process of reconciliation with others – and oneself. For there is an understandable hesitancy to let the past simply slip away, without acknowledgement of guilt; and a justifiable belief that to do so would constitute an act of betrayal.

Two years of reporting (as Antjie Samuel) with an SABC radio team on the Truth and Reconciliation Commission's hearings resulted in Antjie Krog's *Country of my Skull* (Random House). Written unlike her poetry in English and packed with horrifying detail and confessional, this prose work is part documentary, part oddly fictionalised personal narrative. At one point, in one side of a constructed dialogue, she posits: 'Maybe writers in S. Africa should shut up for a while . . . let the domain rather belong to those who literally paid blood for every faltering word they utter before the Truth Commission'.

Against this the writer's challenge is, in the face of dark events, to salute the human spirit: the danger otherwise a failure to take possession of their own history. The title poem of Gus Ferguson's deliciously ingenious *Light Verse at the end of the Tunnel* (David Phillip) wittily suggests death needn't end things but 'is, as mystics all contend/An ultimate caesura'. The term perhaps helpfully defines where South African poetry finds itself: a breakpoint for fruitful self-examination, yet emphatically indicating a continuing. And what right have we to expect miracles overnight in literature, any more than in life?

Don Maclennan is a humane sceptic very much in the Norman MacCaig mould. Born in London in 1929 and educated at Witwatersrand and Edinburgh, he taught English and Philosophy until retiring in 1994 from Rhodes University. Very much South Africa's senior practitioner in English, Maclennan and his poetry gleam with a lucid intelligence and integrity, most recently in *Solstice* (Snailpress/Scottish Cultural Press). His free forms are honed with such craft as to seem pre-ordained. In the face of their rather relentlessly pessimistic testimony to mortality he believes love to be more durable than politics, and that while 'a word may sing like a knife . . . yet imagination heals the wounds of life'. The future of South African poetry in English would seem to hinge on this and other freedoms; on future generations untramelled by any sense of colonial inheritance, loving what can be loved of this still riven and tormented land, in the language of insight, intelligence and compassion.

A number of poets have matured in the wake of Livingstone, Maclennan and Lionel Abrahams (b.1928) – his an erudite poetry of the mind rather than of place or belonging to place, and down the years both impressively and courageously articulate on his own 'shackling' through physical disability, as within the wider context of an oppressive regime. But they tended to be muted, obscured even, in the prevailing clangour. For them to come into their own would be fitting and salutary. A prerequisite is for the nerve-centre of the poetry to be intensely personal, concerned with the intimacies of human existence rather than subservient to dogma.

Jeremy Cronin has certainly been heard. He studied at Cape Town and Paris, then returned to South Africa and worked for the ANC until arrested in 1976 and sentenced to seven years imprisonment. *Inside* (Ravan Press) unleashes a political rage – but also contains finely crafted love poems to his first wife who died of a brain tumour while he was in prison. A second collection *Even the Dead* (David Phillip/Mayibuye) underscores his political convictions and urges solidarity. A sequence entitled 'Moorings' again reveals a more intimate and lyrical impulse. But the structure of the volume underscores an awkward dichotomy of style and content, and I think unevenness.

Born in 1951 Ingrid de Kok is the Director of Extra-Mural Studies at the University of Cape Town. Her second collection *Transfer* (Snailpress) acknowledges the need to put down markers, not least in a land with a shaky memory. But her preferred mode is to see the wide canvas of national events past and present, through an intuitive prism, diurnal and familial. In this merging her strength lies. Observations and memories retain delicacy of feeling and subjectivity without being trapped into the self-referential. Enhancing this are a clarity of insight, and a finesse with language and the shaping and rhyming of a stanza, allied to succulence of sound and image.

Above all, her testimonies of loss and hope resonate or hover imaginatively, so that they speak to and for the returning exile in each of us; not exclusively or stridently for a single group or cause. This applies not least to her probing of what the book's jacket calls 'the slow and painful processes of commemoration and invention that attend reconstruction'. 'Mending' ends:

> *The woman plies her ancient art.*
> *Her needle sutures as it darts,*
> *scoring, scripting, scarring, stitching,*
> *the invisible mending of the heart.*

This is analogous to the healing function of poetry. Part of the artist's role may well be retrospective, as keeper of the communal conscience. Sad though, if that were to stifle tremors relating to the life ahead. Each poet of the future must first and foremost be true to his or her moral self, while attuned to transition and taking language to the limit. It will be fascinating how those to come surmount and transcend not only the legacy of the past, but their own and their country's still far from predictable future. By way of a dictum, they could do worse than the ending of Don Maclennan's 'Letter in a Bottle':

> *All I've ever wanted to make –*
> *a few clean statements*
> *of love and death,*
> *things you cannot fake.*

FUNERALS
[FOR DON MACLENNAN]

You come across as Quixote
tilting at the Man with the Scythe
who reversing the natural
order, has frenziedly
done good friends down.

Your letters tell of orations,
shock of loss, and despair;
at last, consoling arms.
As for love, how answer
its why's and wherefore's?

Enough to say I too fear
the threat of loneliness
without it. And pray
those loved most dearly
find death painless.

Today my steps lead me
through Warriston cemetery,
its unkempt headstones
nullifying any solace
poetry might offer.

Oh for a small son's innocence
who at such abundance
of skulls and crossbones,
asked why so many pirates
had settled in this place.

Glasgow W2

For me there are three Glasgows. I was born and lived in Hillhead till I was almost six. After growing up in Ayrshire – my other 'dear green place' – I returned to stay and work for 20 years in that sector of the city now post-coded G12 but then W2. During my subsequent years in Edinburgh those haunts have come to seem something of a fiction: due in part to the massive changes that have occurred but also because while I still revisit the city there are aspects of its modernity I tend now to see less with my own eyes than through those of writers from the past who have come into their own – and others of a younger generation.

With Byres Road as its spine and the University and the BBC like pit bings one at either end, the old W2 remains imprinted on my memory, part grimy sepia and part autumnal umber and ochre. Green and yellow Corporation trams whined and lurched; the Kelvin ran glutinously through the Garrioch Drive gulch and dumped wrecked branches like filthy candelabra on the weir downstream. The whole crumbling area was a vast litter-bin; terraces taken over by the University falling derelict and Mackintosh's house in Southpark Avenue razed to the ground, a workman's axe put to its front door. Further out Great Western Road the boulevard's spacious private gardens and rose-bushes came within a hairsbreadth of being wantonly bulldozed, for an increase in traffic that would never come.

In Maryhill semi-derelict tenements stood out from the surrounding debris, like teeth waiting to be pulled. But we were detached from these and from other more deprived areas – not to mention the sectarian vomitariums of Ibrox and Parkhead. Only when heading south or east were our delicate sensibilities affronted by highrise blocks, obsolescent before they went up. We took visitors to see the hen-run at the Art School, the Cathedral's stained glass windows and Provand's Lordship, and to Kelvingrove Gallery and Pollok House – skirting rather than crossing the concrete wasteland the city centre had become. Our lives in our middle-class ghetto seemed vital yet oddly cocooned – almost charmed.

Those were the days of yellow pea-soupers: handkerchiefs folded as protective masks, and scarcely seeing a hand at arm's length in front of you. The little red underground trundled round and round like a toy train, the gusty stations with their distinctive tunnel-smell which could have been bottled for exiles. There were occasional dreaded visits to the Western Infirmary with its corridors and boiler-room décor. More often, to the Salon Cinema. Its ticket-kiosk used to open only moments before the film started smack on 5.30. Even if there was a queue the projectionist wouldn't wait. It might've been years before we realised there were such things as opening titles.

Adjoining were the Western Baths directly opposite which, in Cranworth Street, I'd been born. My parents lived in a top flat there while my father was minister of Kelvinside Old. I went back many years later and found that the name on the doorplate was R.C. Risk: he'd have enjoyed that. A stone's throw away were the Botanic Gardens, the Silver Slipper Café on the corner – and further up, across from the old Queen Margaret College, the Kibble Palace.

John Kibble owned the biggest camera in the world. He built the Palace in 1863, on his estate at Coulport on Loch Long. Shortly after, it was transferred to its present site, and enlarged. To begin with it housed concerts and entertainments. Collections of potted plants were laid out and on an island in a pond under the central dome, an orchestra would entertain Kibble's guests. In 1881 the lease was bought out and it was planted more or less as it is today. In 1891 the Corporation of Glasgow took over.

My first piece of land was a section of flower-bed outside it, which some gardener or parkie pretended to give me. No doubt he hung on to plant-picking rights. There I was wheeled in my pram, in my earliest years. I don't know how much I genuinely remember, or how much was inserted in the mind's eye by hearsay – or old photographs: these in turn contributing (and applying a time-scale) to many of my poems.

Queen Margaret College for Girls had long before been transformed into the main Scottish broadcasting centre. Here I became, as Dylan Thomas put it, one of those young men who seeking adventure ran away to the BBC. Television was still in its infancy. Radio ruled the roost. From studio management I gravitated to production. My office was variously a fungus-ridden basement in Buckingham Terrace, perhaps symbolically below the Religious Department; a hut on what had been a bowling-green; an attic glory-hole; and latterly, a room overlooking a little courtyard with its still preserved Rennie Mackintosh tower and weather-vane.

For a while I shared a top-floor flat on the far side of the Kelvin owned by violinist Peter Gibbs, leader of the BBC Scottish Symphony Orchestra. In 'the palace' as we called it, we blanched at him doing carpentry, an electric saw millimetres from his fingers. Years later Peter, a former air ace, mysteriously disappeared while up in a small plane.

A strapping horn-player lived below us, seemingly in a cardboard box in his front room: we never found out if this was an acoustic cubicle or a fall-out shelter. Friends' flats our milieu, life was a colourful caravanserai of writers, painters and composers. A real excitement since has been observing so many of them find renown in Scotland and beyond: none more (or more deservedly) than those extravagantly gifted twin peaks James Kelman and Alasdair Gray, the latter's output then ranging from distinctive portraits and line-drawings to Elizabethan-style sonnets, radio plays and prose pieces which would in time be incorporated in *Lanark*.

In the early '60s the BBC Club had transferred from a semi-derelict Hyndland station to Botanic Crescent. No sooner were the new premises refurbished, than dry rot was discovered: one evening a Welsh sound technician fell through the loo. There were the nearby howffs, from the Curlers and the Rubaiyat down Byres Road, to the Pewter Pot with its Guinness froth and tang of stale urine.

My first stage play, hammered out on my father's old Underwood, had been in five acts. I showed it to no one, and burned it. It was a joy to discover I needn't tackle anything so long again. In 1961 the Citizens' premiered *Break Down*: the Orpheus and Eurydice story set in an espresso-bar, with an underground station and tunnel as the entrance to Hades. For *I Didn't Always Live Here* (1967), set in a Govan tenement and an old woman's memory, Jack House wrote a programme note. I never got to know him but still remember bumping into him one day and observing,

'You're in a hurry, Jack.' 'I'm going to a funeral,' he replied. All I could blurt out was, 'Oh, I'm sorry . . . no one close, I hope?' 'My wife . . . '.

The University Arts Theatre Group provided a congenial outlet as, from early married days in a tiny top-floor 'eyebrows' flat in Belhaven Terrace to the close-knit yet cosmopolitan flavour of Hamilton Drive, perspectives and time-scales juxtaposed and overlapped. One constant was the Kibble Palace: birds flitting among tree-ferns; water-drops exquisitely looping from sprinklers; snoozing old men sub-aqueous in its clammy tropicality. No longer just a physical reference point it seemed increasingly a repository for my family tree – mirroring the passage of the generations.

In the same wartime raid as had pock-marked the granite of Queen Margaret Bridge my nursery school across the river was hit by a bomb and one of the teachers killed. I remember making things with grey modelling clay (this before coloured plasticine) and baking loaves like figures-of-eight. At least I think I do.

Later during my adult stay there two women in Edwardian dresses, with parasols, used to walk to and fro or stand for hours outside the men's Union. The story was that they were a mother and daughter, one having been betrayed by a medical student. They were ghostly figures. I hoped there might be a happy ending, but heard later that both had been put away.

My wife and I were fortunate in forming warm (and enduring) friendships among our neighbours; a stimulating cross-section spanning the arts and sciences, medicine and academe, and with many a maverick among them. John Purser was a figure of vast energy and endowed with an impressive range of strings to his bow. Over and above his considerable reputation in the fields of literature and music, he would later make an influential contribution to our culture through *Scotland's Music*. While there remains a creative Radio Scotland (which in the wake of Birt's destructiveness, and with things here as pusillanimous as they are, some fear may not be long) his broadcast series must remain one of its crowning glories. More personally and over many years, I am fortunate to have been one of the many to find him inspirational, generous-spirited, the ideal host and an exhilarating (if not undemanding) guide to routes not just up the Cuillin but for heart and mind to explore.

Except during the Fair when it traditionally tended to pour, Glasgow had sporadic hot spells. Then everyone would stream into the Botanics: young couples intertwined or pushing prams, families picnicking and attendants blowing whistles as errant children stumbled across the lawn in pursuit of the pigeons. The sun always seemed unexpected, catching folk unawares, shirt-sleeves incongruously rolled or jackets dangling. Even on ordinary days there were images and sounds for the garnering: schoolboys in cherry caps and corduroys crossing Great Western Road, the keeper heading to the hothouse to be with his orchids and marble nudes; one artist neighbour wobbling on the cobbles of our back lane, on a penny-farthing; another heading for his studio, in leather boots and sombrero. At the gates of the Gardens, the winnowing fantails would preen and pirouette. In the main glass-house the arrow on the banana-tree would still point precariously upwards, to its lone fruit.

Time passes. The shades of grey caught by Oscar Marzaroli's camera and the skelly children so colourfully preserved by Joan Eardley become ever more distant fragments of a continuous archive. More brutalist images and installations are housed in the new Gallery of Modern Art – formerly the Royal Exchange and Stirling's Library (and incorporating the 18th century mansion of an Ayrshire-born tobacco lord, William Cunninghame). Initially the choice of pieces and their setting put the cat among those pouting pigeons, Edinburgh's self-appointed arbiters of taste. Meanwhile Dalí's glossy Christ of St John of the Cross, cause of such a furore in the '50s, still hangs – the sales of cards and artefacts having recouped its cost many times over.

The statues fronting the old Citizens' Theatre building have found other homes, and the pillared façade has gone. But the directorial triumverate, with their 'band of gypsies' so demonised for '*decadence*' in the '70s, were to become bedecked pillars of the community. A sea-change on the literary and socio-cultural scene has been its Kelmanisation, and the lingering ambivalence towards this writer of (to me) bold vision, dark wit and profound humanity. In a wider context Glasgow was 1990 European City of Culture: the subsequent concern being the loss or dissipation of energy and what the city and its people had accrued.

Decades ago the trams disappeared for good. So with the coming of the Clyde Tunnel, then the Kingston Bridge, did the Clyde ferries. I remember Finnieston and Govan best, like frames in a strip-cartoon. Once when I was the only person waiting I rang a big bell on a post, which I assumed was to let the ferry know you were there. When eventually it sluiced in a man came bounding off it and thrust his nose close to mine: 'That's the fucken fog-bell, jimmy!'

Crossing on another miserable night were a couple like Andy Capp and Florrie. Wailing, she clambered onto the gunwale and stood precariously balanced. While everyone tensed, he puffed away at his fag. At the other side she got down, still weeping. He threw his dowt into the water. As they disappeared towards Partick cross we heard: 'Cum affit wumman, ye hud nae intention!'

It's not so very long since the intonation of Partick and Govan, north and south of the river, could in the shipyards be finely differentiated and a bone of contention: 'It's nothin to do wi you – you're no' a Govan man.' The specific imprint of the west end perpetuates its own snobberies and fierce antipathies. On a number of occasions I sensed in a pub sneer or reviewer's gibe an implied 'You're middle-class' – i.e. not a real Weegie (as in a wider context but as challengingly, if you don't toe a particular party line – whether linguistic or political – not a true Scot).

After my enforced departure to Edinburgh there was no point in even a token rejoinder. I was beyond the pale. That my heart was still in the west, though my head in the east, was to no avail: the chasm, in terms of social perception, was insuperable – and absolute. Columnist Frank Keating neatly encapsulated this. In Scotland to cover a title-bout at the St Andrew's Hall and a Five Nations international at Murrayfield, and asked why he was here, he'd reply, 'For the fight and the match.' In Glasgow they asked what match; in Edinburgh which fight?

My own favourite come-uppance hit me out of the blue. In the bus back into the city centre after a writers' workshop at Carnwadric a woman animatedly and amicably said how much she'd enjoyed things, and had learned from the others. As we crossed the river she got up saying it was her stop, and asked how far I was going. I said Queen Street. 'No, I mean where are you from?' I explained I was going back to Edinburgh. She was absolutely gob-smacked. The bus jolted to a stop. As the doors swished shut she screwed up her features and cackled like a harpy: *'Haw, we fair pipped youse fur the architecture!'*

DEPARTURE

Once in Dumbarton Road
we passed an antique shop
crammed with grandfather clocks:

by the time we decided
to buy one, they'd gone
in a shipment to America.

An opportunity missed.
Yet what does it matter —
one grandfather surely

much like another. So
I tell myself, when I think
of them shoulder to shoulder.

Now I too
have been long away;
nothing in my face

or resonance of strike,
to proclaim
or betray my origin.

Despite that I retain,
like them, an ingrained
sense of belonging —

though in my case
a steady heartbeat,
not a pendulum swing.

The Forest of Ettrick

This was the title of a feature I once produced for a radio series called 'Pride of Place'. The songs and ballad extracts were sung by Archie Fisher. I can still hear his wonderfully lucid delivery of them.

> *Ettrick Foreste is a fair foreste,*
> *   In it grows many a seemly tree;*
> *There's hart and hynde, and roe and doe,*
> *   And of all wild beastis great plentie.*
>
> *There an Outlaw keeps five hundred men,*
> *   He keeps a royal companie.*
> *His merry men are in livery clad,*
> *   Of the forest green so fair to see;*
> *He and his ladye in purple clad,*
> *   Oh! if they live not royallie.*
>
> *Word is gane to our noble King*
> *   In Edinburgh where that he lay,*
> *That there was this outlaw in Ettrickside*
> *   Counted him for nocht, nor all his countrie.*

Ettrick Forest is the ancient name for the Sheriffdom of Selkirkshire, in the heart of the Scottish Borderland. It has been claimed that the Outlaw was John Murray, herdsman in this land of feuding and defiance in the 1460s – and the King he was confronting, James IV:

> *'Thir lands are mine' the Outlaw said,*
>   *'I ken nae king in Christentie;*
> *Frae Soudron I this foreste won,*
>   *When the king and his knights were not to see.*
>
> *'Fair Philiphaugh is mine by right,*
>   *And Lewinshope still mine shall be;*
> *Newark, Foulshiells, and Tinnies baith*
>   *My bow and arrow purchased me . . .*
>
> *'But I'll give to thee my castel keys,*
>   *With the blessings of my fair ladye,*
> *Gin thou'llt mak me sherrif of this Foreste*
>   *And all my offspring after me.'*
>
> *The keys of the castel he gave the King,*
>   *Wi' the blessing of his fair ladye;*
> *He was made sherrif of Ettrick Foreste,*
>   *Surely while upward grows the tree;*
> *And if he was na traitor to the King*
>   *Forfaulted he suld never be.*
>
> *Wha ever heard, in ony time,*
>   *Sicken an outlaw in his degree,*
> *Sic favour get before a King,*
>   *As did the Outlaw Murray of the Forest frie?*

– THE OUTLAW MURRAY –

The Forest originally embraced the valleys of Ettrick and Yarrow, which meet just south of Selkirk, and Tweed, into which they flow. It was known in early times as *Ecclesia de Foresta* or *Rectoria de Foresta*, the monks of Dryburgh being granted the patronage of the 'Kirks of the Blessed Virgin Mary, in Ettrick Forest'. The Exchequer Rolls dating from 1264 describe it as 'a Royal Forest well replenished with wild boar and other game'. Granted to the Douglas family by Robert the Bruce it reverted to the crown in the mid-15th century and became a favourite hunting ground of the Scottish kings and famed for the largest stags in the land. The crest of the Dukes of Buccleuch (*buck-cleuch*) was a stag trippant with horns and hoofs of gold.

After Flodden where the pride of Border manhood, the Flowers o' the Forest, fell James V gave the surviving souters (shoemakers) of Selkirk freedom to cut down what wood was needed to rebuild their town. Freebooting led to more destruction. Ettrick became a vast sheepwalk.

Though I was born and brought up in the west my mother's father Robert Russell Stewart was from Selkirk and named after the Rev. James Russell, minister of Yarrow in the late 19th century. His maternal grandfather, a shepherd in Ettrick, is buried in the local kirkyard. With this (and a couple of trout-rods) as incentive I decided to spend a few days on the upper reaches of Ettrick, to see if I might sense any resonance of place – or ancestry.

I arrived on an evening in mid-May. As I drove the last stretch the road, unravelling and narrowing, kept close to the river, its waters muddy and swirling at first but becoming milky, then clear, and revealing the valley cradled rather than hemmed in by the hills. Early next morning there was a bright mist. I could see clumps of daffodils, a cherry thrusting through, a thrush sitting on eggs in a tree at the corner of a drystane dyke, a cock-pheasant perched imperiously (but it seemed precariously) on a gatepost. On the slopes opposite sheep grazed.

Ettrick Water rises in a mossy seepage and merging of hill-streams, in a broad half-circle of curlew-country comprising Capel Fell, Wind Fell and Ettrick Pen, each over 2,000 feet. Its course captivated James Brown whose poems, including 'an exile's letter home from Canada' after he'd emigrated, were written under the pen-name J.B. Selkirk:

> *Gie me a border burn*
> *That canna rin without a turn,*
> *And wi' its bonnie babble fills*
> *The glens amang oor native hills.*
> *How men that ance have kenn'd aboot it*
> *Can leeve their after-lives without it*
> *I canna tell, for day and nicht*
> *It comes unca'd for to my sicht.*

Is there a bonnier bit
On any water, head to fit,
Where, tumblin' doon the rugged streams,
The lashing water froths and creams,
Till o'er the saumon-loup it spins
Tween green Heimburn and Kirkhope linns,
Where Ettrick rins?
     Then past Brigend
And fair Howford it taks a bend,
And wanders through wi' gentler turn
The quiet haughs o' Hutlerburn;
Then on its way it gi'es a ca'
At Fauldshope, Aikwood, Carterha . . .

    – 'Epistle to Tammas' –

In 1645 at Philiphaugh, where Ettrick and Yarrow meet, Montrose's
Royalists were surprised and slaughtered almost to a man, by the
Covenanters under General Leslie. The adjacent stretch of pasture-land is
the site of one of the oldest and eeriest of Border tales:

O I forbid you, maidens a',
   That wear gowd in your hair,
To come or gae by Carterhaugh,
   For young Tam Lin is there.

For even about that knight's middle,
   O' silver bells are nine;
And nae maid goes to Carterhaugh,
   And a maid returns again.

Despite fair warning Janet seeks out Tam Lin, and in due course bears his
child. Desperate to return to her and to humankind he explains that to
disenchant him she must return alone at *the mirk and midnight hour* on All
Hallow's Eve, when the fairy folk will ride:

O first let pass the black, lady,
   And syne let pass the brown,

But quickly run to the milk-white steed,
    Pu' ye his rider down.

They'll turn me in your arms, lady,
    Into an esk and vile adder;
But hold me fast, and fear me not,
    For I am your bairn's father.

They'll turn me to a bear sae grim,
    And then a lion bold;
But hold me fast, and fear me not,
    As ye shall love your child.

Again they'll turn me in your arms
    To a red hot gaud of airn;
But haud me fast, and fear me not,
    For I'll do to you no harm.

And last they'll turn me in your arms
    Into the burning gleed;
Then throw me into well water,
    0 throw me in wi speed.

And then I'll be your ain true love,
    I'll turn a naked knight;
Then cover me wi your green mantle,
    And cover me out o sight.'

And when they changed him in her arms
    Into a naked man;
She's thrown her mantle him abune,
    And true love she has won.

Out then spak the Fairy Queen
    And an angry woman was she,
'She's ta'en away the bonniest knight
    In a' my companie.

Adieu, Tam Lin! But gin I kent
A ladye had borrow'd thee,
I wad ta'en out thy twa grey e'en,
Put in twa o' wood o' the tree.'

– 'TAM LIN' –

At Ettrickhall a monument marks the birthplace of James Hogg, the 'Ettrick Shepherd'. Contemporary and friend if at times the butt of Scott (with whom he tramped the hills, seeking material for his Border Minstrelsy) Hogg is best-known for his poems and stories and his lowering masterpiece *The Private Memoirs and Confessions of a Justified Sinner.* Carlyle saw him as 'a little red-skinned, stiff sack of a body [with] a highish though sloping brow (among his yellow grizzled hair), and two clear little beads of blue or grey eyes that sparkle, if not with thought, yet with animation'.

No doubt something of the sparkle disappeared the night he tried, after a drinking bout with his cronies, to loup over his wall-eyed pony and fell, breaking his nose! The shepherd bard who 'taught the wandering winds to sing', and who turned down Scott's offer of a ticket for George IV's coronation because it clashed with the St Boswell's sheep fair, is buried here in Ettrick's little kirkyard – scarcely a stone's throw from where he was born. The circle complete. Adjoining Hogg's simple headstone is that of his grandfather 'the far-famed Will o' Phaup, who for feats of frolic, agility and strength had no equal in his day'.

In the top corner, on the last stone I came to, are marked in clear lettering – among the Napiers and Laidlaws – three generations of Donaldsons, including John Donaldson, who died at Yarrow in 1868 aged 82, and his mother who died at Hopehouse, Ettrick, in her 92nd year. My great-great-great grandmother, she was born in 1747, within a year of Culloden. Nestling at the foot of the stone is a carved dove. Hard to describe my feelings, as I ponder these ties of the blood. It's as though some element within me had been somehow resolved, put at rest, in this little kirkyard nestling amidst the soft contours of the Border hills. The whole setting redolent of life and – as in the last stanza of Lady John Scott's poem – loss:

When I last rade down Ettrick,
The winds were shifting, the storm was waking,

The snow was drifting, my heart was breaking,
For we never again were to ride thegither,
In sun or storm on the mountain heather,
    When I last rade down Ettrick.

– 'ETTRICK' –

Ettrick, not wild as it can be but dappled in sunlight, is balm to the spirit. On this hill-burn above Shorthope, a startled roebuck dashing through the trees; or climbing between Buccleuch and Deloraine, the Eildons in the distance. Not every temperament can sustain peacefulness. For those who do, this spot must be perfect. Hogg again:

I thought the hills were sharp as knives,
    An' the braid lift lay whomel'd on them,
An' glowered wi' wonder at the wives
    That spak o' ither hills ayon them.

As ilka year gae something new,
    Addition to my mind or stature,
So fast my love for Ettrick grew,
    Implanted in my very nature.

– 'FAREWELL TO ETTRICK' –

A sense of ancestry surely implies an empathy with the past and towards a particular place that has been, for a spell at least, the centre of the world. Once *implanted* this can never be wholly excised. Pride of place would seem inseparable too from a pride in its people: here, a sturdy local stock. John Buchan praised the Border shepherd's independence and tolerance. There also seems a prevailing courtesy and gravity.

The Borders have had attributed to them a permanence of mind. This isn't surprising. In any threatened territory or debatable land, self-containment and durability are needed for survival. Paradoxically resistance to change can be undermined not just by the imposition of a new order but through the reinstatement of an old. There have been big changes, mainly through forestry making a come-back in the '60s and '70s. Thousands of sheep went out of Ettrick and Eskdalemuir to make way for trees. The bulk of the shepherds left too, I was told, making the houses empty: 'It was good hill ground they were taking, a lot of them just city people with money jouking the income tax. They plant them and bring squads from Langholm and Lockerbie to look after them now and again. It's coming back, the Ettrick Forest's coming back'.

But there was nothing of the beauty of the ancient birch forest; too much of the planting being uniform and dully predictable. Fortunately Nature's variety remains; habitat for oyster-catcher, mallard and goosander, white-bibbed dippers and whirring wheatear. As well as one unwanted reiver, mink, much on the increase. And unexpected excitements – like the pair of peregrine falcon spiralling over me, as I stand on this rocky ridge.

Ettrick, starred with primroses; Yarrow, its mellowness admired by Wordsworth; and Tweed, more luscious still, its glistening waters skirting the ruins of the graceful Border abbeys . . . Each has a distinctive character yet complements the others, contributing to an over-all expression of continuity. Potential for magic and minstrelsy. And for those who seek it, solitude. But not total: the roar of jet-planes constantly heightening, in this environment, an awareness of the threat overhanging ourselves and our children.

As for my genealogy, and pride in it . . . these remain real. Though *pride* is too intractable for something with such shifts and shades of meaning and for which in any case I can take no credit. Some links, however selective, remain. Others have been long severed. It isn't possible, so briefly or even over longer spells not contributing towards the economics of a place, to step back into a discarded skin. Even as it moulds us the present becomes the past and remains, however we try to conjure it up, irretrievable.

NEAR MOREBATTLE

'See that brown and white heifer on the far hill —
when the horizontal lines meet along the back and belly,
you fire. With a rifle like that you should hit
a stag in the neck at a quarter of a mile —
even the Army'd find that hard to beat.' Out at three
in the morning he'd brought back the carcass of a deer
and the brush of a dog fox — knowing he was there
from a sudden rankness in the dewy air . . .

That night I take my new trout-rod for a try-out
upstream from where we are staying. Soon
it is too dark even to tie a blood-knot,
or do more than sense in what pool I am casting.
On the way back I hear footsteps on iron.
Three men bar the bridge. 'Caught anything?
The whitling should be up before long,
worth waiting for . . . What are you fishing,

dry fly? Better with worm. See you then.'
They smile, and disappear. Able to hear
only the water rippling on its stones, I picture
both sides of a very different border
where the snapping of twigs carries its own terror.
How lucky, that we can bring our children here,
to accessible streams untainted with fear,
and hills resplendent in their wearing of the green.

From the Wilderness

ALASDAIR MACLEAN

Big-built and soft-spoken, Alasdair Maclean dedicated himself to a life's journey as rigorous as it was to become solitary. Born in Glasgow in 1926 he left school at 14. After a spell in the Clyde shipyards he did National Service at sea and in the Dardanelles, was with the British and Indian Armies, then worked as a laboratory technician in London and Canada. His roving days over he became a mature student at Edinburgh University. His father had retired prematurely from the Clyde Navigation Trust to the family croft at Sanna, on the bleak finger of rock of which Maclean wrote *'God was short of earth when He made Ardnamurchan'* ('Stone'). Not till he was in his forties, unknown but for winning a BBC students' poetry competition, did he burst fully-armed on the literary scene.

In 1969 a group of his poems appeared in *Lines Review*. A Faber selection followed. An SAC bursary subsequently enabled him to complete *From the Wilderness* (Gollancz, 1973). Critically acclaimed it was a Poetry Book Society Choice and won the Duff Cooper Memorial Prize. Its prefatory poem 'To the Reader' moves from the uncompromising '*I am not bondsman to your least shout, / nor friend; perhaps if I could choose, more foe*' to the more conciliatory '*Meet me at the point where language bends*'.

Other poems in the volume might be hewn from the bedrock of

Ardnamurchan. They contain honed descriptions (some corralled from other poets) of animals in their habitat. Set against distrust of Nature was a oneness with the Seasons and a land that 'rocks at its anchor'. Despite the long shadows of Heaney and Hughes his perceptions were his own, his metaphors powerful, each phrase pursuing the poem's aim. He could marvel, or be sardonic – as when he and his father appeared in the *Scottish Field* in

> *a photograph so clear*
> *you could count the midges.*
> Highland peasants cutting peat.
> The abundance of free fuel
> is an important factor in the crofting economy.
> *One of my father's rare grim smiles,*
> *like a lull in the east wind,*
> *broke out when I read that to him.*
>
> – 'AT THE PEATS' –

As the book progresses, and the calendar year draws to a close, it becomes more deeply personal and pessimistic. In 1973 both his parents died – predeceased I believe, by a brother. *Waking the Dead* (1976) contained a sequence of metrically formal elegies for his mother. The other poems were freer and struck a note of gallows-humour jauntiness. The prefatory poem this time ended 'Beyond me there are monsters. Real ones.': the greatest of these, the carnivore Death. The volume was to his dismay much less favourably received.

Night Falls on Ardnamurchan (1984), also from Gollancz, is an illuminating prose commentary on his background and the twilight of a crofting community. Painfully and lovingly it shows his father's simplicity yet complexity, alongside evocative description and a heartrending, at times scathing record of the passing of a bitterly embraced way of life. Its stoicism is leavened by gleams of beauty; moments of lightness and paradox. Angered by mockery of the Highlander which 'in the guise of comedy, has a long and dishonest tradition in print', he berates the tourist mentality and influx of 'white settlers'; then chastises as scathingly the inertia of the indigenous crofters whose scapegoating of the Clearances, for all their ills, he sees as 'a fatal charm'. If his poems are stepping-stones to this book, it in turn glosses and illumines them.

On finding four of his poems in *The Faber Book of Twentieth-Century Scottish Poetry* he wrote in protest to *The Scotsman* that having told his agents to handle such matters without reference to him, he now regretted his lack of concern:

> Had I known, I would certainly have refused permission. May I use a little of your space to make it clear that I disagree profoundly with Mr Dunn's nationalist stance and am appalled at being made to appear a willing soldier in his ranks. I have asked Faber to remove my work from future editions.

Other letters to the editor on the issue conformed more to type by bemoaning omissions from the anthology: an editor's lot is not a happy one. As for Maclean's gesture, I can't but feel he was cutting off his nose to spite his face; or at any rate blurring the line between integrity and thrawnness. At the same time I respected his refusal to be as he saw it a place-man.

We'd first met when he came to Edinburgh to record some poems for a radio selection I was producing. George Macbeth, doyen of London poetry producers, happened to be in the canteen. I asked Alasdair if he'd like to join us for a coffee. Many a man would have been up the stairs like a shot. He gruffly declined, said he had shopping to do and left, a crumpled *New Statesman* sticking from his overcoat pocket. I suspect this reflected both his reclusiveness and an unreadiness to cow-tow or seek favours. For all that, he took critical rebuke hard.

While working as a librarian in Kirkcaldy he wrote *Coming to Grief,* a fantasy for radio with Grief the railway terminus to which we all gravitate; where we end up, in our spiritual autobiography. It tapped a wide range of accents and registers, from ululating Negro women at a mock trial to the narrator as a tear-spattered small boy, then disillusioned old soldier. The play ended with a gunshot, signalling his suicide.

His next play for radio was set during World War II. A first draft I felt was cliché'd and duplicated existing plays. When I regretfully told him I didn't believe it was acceptable or would do his reputation justice, he announced that he would return the commission-fee – until persuaded that not only was this not expected of him, but that I knew of no machinery to cope. I strongly urged him to write another play – but although we exchanged further letters I don't remember our meeting again.

Later poems of his which I came across I found fluent and finely crafted.

Some in an anonymous shortlist for a *TLS* competition suggested a buoyancy unclouded by the undercurrents of personal bleakness, touching on misanthropy, which had previously seemed so much his hallmark. How good if there were enough from the intervening 18 years for another book, to round things off. I am led to believe a manuscript exists but that whether through financial over-expectancy or protectiveness on the part of his executor or legal representatives, this has to date been neither published nor lodged in a library where it could be accessible for reference and research purposes.

Behind my writing this there lies an additional curiosity. In 1966 Longmans of London had published *The Field of Sighing, a Highland Boyhood* by Donald Angus Cameron: a highly readable and informative account of life in a remote highland community. According to the blurb the author 'attended the local township school, and at fourteen became a shepherd on the mountain farm rented by his farmer. At seventeen he joined the Merchant Navy in which he has been ever since, except for a spell as a lumberjack in British Columbia and a year on a Venezuelan plantation.'

Sons of El Dorado: Venezualan adventure (Harlow, Longmans, 1968) by D.A. Cameron is listed on the Eureka world-wide database, as a work of description and travel, with drawings by Peter Edwards. It and *The Field of Sighing* are the author's only works in the Bodleian. Despite the latter having been reprinted in 1981 my attempts to track down the author or unearth anything further on him through the publishers, potential funding bodies, newspaper articles or private sources, have drawn a complete blank: he seems to have vanished into thin air. This whetted my interest in the affinities – and dissimilarities – between it and Maclean's (much more richly poetic) *Ardnamurchan Journal.*

Cameron's book gives his family home as Blarosnich: *blàr* with *osnaich*, his 'field of sighing'. Other local names are in Gaelic. Maclean's are in English. While the blurb states that Cameron was born in 1925, the database extends this to '1925 or '26': the latter, it so happens, Maclean's year of birth. The two volumes are themselves accounts of consecutive decades in the lifespan of their authors: one would fit, that's to say, as a chronological sequel to the other in a continuous depiction of the decline of a crofting community. Beyond this Cameron says his father kept a daily diary; while much of Maclean's book draws on terse extracts from his father's daily journal, selected from identical (but arbitrary) dates in 1960 and 1970. Cameron bemoans writing poor poetry. Maclean the saturnine nature-poet had a late flowering – but concedes he started at the age of twenty.

Tone, syntax and Maclean's sustained intensity aside, there are marked differences. Cameron has few literary allusions; Maclean ranges from the O'Rahilly and Francis Thomson to Housman. While Cameron condemns those who 'had denied their trust and gone off to the gutters of London and Paris squandering the large portion the Lord above had given them', he shows none of Maclean's rancour. A pivotal presence in Cameron is his grandmother, Herself: Maclean does not echo this. Nor does he pursue the occupants of the Big House as Cameron does: ultimately the two women become pitiful figures, cutting themselves off after learning how the locals deride them.

Then there is the labour. Cameron described how to make a scythe and names its component parts; Maclean details the practice and dangers of scything only to end up flinging the implement aside as he flees the midges. Again with sheep and their habits and diseases: Cameron lists the ravages of blowfly, whereas Maclean shows a sense of the ridiculous. I enjoy the thought of him seeing a tame sheep jump up and down at the coming of spring, then looking round to make sure no one is there and (sheepishly) doing likewise.

It is within the family however that the greatest differences lie. An only son, Cameron describes his mother's death in childbirth, then her burning mattress setting fire to hay in the yard. Tension mounts between him and his father when the latter is seen embracing Betty, the landgirl – whom he marries. Compare Maclean, with brothers and a sister, and the impact of both parents' deaths within so short a period. Hurt lingers too, when he tells his mother he has got only a Second at Edinburgh, and she cuttingly replies, 'It's no' as good as a First, is it?'

Not the least intriguing feat, were both books from the one pen, would be this degree of differentiation between them, for all their common ground. Consistent too with an 'incognito' theory might be the notion of the dramatic events involving Cameron's parents actually being a cunning disguise: and (as such) among the 'highly-coloured and semi-fictional' accounts of highland life Maclean later deplores in his Prologue.

Against this, there would arise the whole question of Maclean having so successfully covered his tracks. And in the absence of counter-evidence it seems churlish if not downright fatuous to dispute Gollancz's categorical claim (though even this, I suppose, needn't be conclusive) that *Night Falls in Ardnamurchan* was his 'first non-fiction book'.

It is hard on the other hand to believe that Maclean wouldn't have been aware of the other book's existence. In this context their dissimilarity takes on further significance: there is emphatically no least whiff of plagiarism. One nice nuance fuels any lingering notion of intrigue. Maclean's dust-jacket has a colour photo; Cameron's croft painting is unattributed. Maclean moreover provides a neat drawing of his croft and its environs. The Pathfinder Map confirms its accuracy. It also shows, just out of frame and little over a mile to the south on the road to Kilchoan, a clutch of houses with the name Achosnich: from (this time) *achadh* and *osnaich*, a variant for Field of Sighing. A little further to the south-east and on the coastline, as if cocking a snook at all this, is 'Maclean's Nose'.

Whether there is a mystery to unravel is in any case of less import than the product of his self-styled 'darker side'; and the fate of his uncollected poems. I hope these see the light of day. Like Edwin Muir's and as individually, Alasdair Maclean's poetry perceives people and places, and a remote way of life, in such a way as to probe the significance of human existence.

As in Muir a God is omnipresent. But Maclean's is a stonier figure, of whom the unforgiving landscape is very much a physical projection. And whereas Muir's accumulated emblems mirror a transfiguring spirituality, Maclean's transformations remain more ominous, their mockery (and self-mockery) amounting at times almost to savagery.

Alasdair Maclean fused internal and external worlds, making the rocks glow in such a way as conveyed not just a shadowed personal history but that of his race. Earthbound he may be. But the closing lines of one poem envisage both physical and metaphysical escape, in a manner which precludes their use on any gravestone:

> *I'd choose the sky for burial*
> *though, if such were possible,*
> *I'd have mountains at my head and feet.*
> *When Gabriel blew his trumpet I'd arrive*
> *before God's kindness became strained.*
> *The clouds would ease my bones*
> *more than the hard rocks of Ardnamurchan.*
> *Not worms would feed on me but larks.*

– 'SEA AND SKY' –

Music and Muse

George Mackay Brown

It was in the '60s and '70s that I saw George Mackay Brown most frequently: in Glasgow or Edinburgh, and on forays to Orkney to record poems or discuss adapting his work for radio; on holiday with my wife; then at his gravely courteous invitation, to read at the St Magnus Festival. In those early days there seemed something imperturbably cherubic about him: a twinkling eye, a wicked gift for mimicry and an unerring compass-bearing on the nearest pint. He gave generously of his time and attention, despite the demands of his admirers and the truffle-hunters already starting to beat a path to his door.

My first Orkney trip was to tape a feature to be presented by the artist Stanley Cursitor – piqued at the *Radio Times* having called him the Queen's *limmer* (rather than *limner*) in Scotland. George was there on the pier to welcome me. He was to introduce me to his dearly trusted (and enduringly hospitable) friends Elizabeth and Archie Bevan; to painter Sylvia Wishart, poet Charlie Senior, sonneteer and naturalist Robert Rendall with his store of religious tomes and *grottiebuckies*, and a swarm of resident writers and artists. Later I'd get to know Gunnie Moberg and Tam McPhail, themselves so close to and supportive of George, especially in his later years.

He took me to the stone-slabbed burial mound of Maeshowe and the

Ring of Brodgar, and across to Hoy and the distilled beauty of Rackwick. He gave me a tour of his beloved St Magnus Cathedral in one of whose beautiful stained-glass windows his lines are now quoted. I felt the mule-kick of his home-brew. He seemed something of a still centre, not one for high-falutin chat: if I asked what something in one of his poems meant, like as not he'd start intoning 'Pied Beauty' or hum a few bars from Beethoven's Ninth.

In those days I'd cross by sea, dreading signs of storm and the St Ola lurching the long way round the east of Hoy. I'll never forget my first drive down the barriers, with George my guide to the Italian chapel at Lamb Holm; a family holiday later near the Palace of Birsay and trying fruitlessly to count the black rabbits on the Broch; or sailing to Sanday, passing Wyre, land and sea quartered as on a shield, alien voices rising in the imagination. Later came the Pier Arts Centre with its boats by Wallis and Hilton, and readings upstairs in the big log-fire room.

Then there were our recording sessions. Readings from *The Storm* and *Loaves and Fishes*, and a sequence entitled 'Stations of the Cross', were added to the body of his work already lodged in the BBC sound archive. George would be increasingly nervous beforehand, as though all the wiles and pitfalls of technology were compressed into the microphone – itself much more bulkily forbidding than today's neat little lapel jobs. More than once after an injection of courage in the hotel bar, a walk had to be taken across the golf course and back along the shore path, to clear our heads for the fray. In due course I'd have the task of getting the clumsily weighty recording gear safely back to base. On one sea-lashed return voyage to Scrabster I feared several tapes-worth of cantos had been damaged by salt water. Another time, one of the precious spools turned out to have nothing on it but snores: I imagine it in the vaults of Buffalo University library: catalogued 'the bard, somnolent'.

Edwin Muir wrote not only of 'the strangeness and magic' of George's early work, but of its containing 'something I can only call grace'. All the more remarkable was its being leavened by a nose for human foible and interest in the ordinariness of people, whatever their station or pretensions. Not one to cow-tow to fashion he retained, without fear or favour, a staunch loyalty to and identification with his place of origin. I suspect too that his lifelong distaste for the limelight went deeper than mere modesty or shyness, but reflected a deep-rooted view of the writer. A lover of the Ballads, he saw them as 'in a real sense the work of an entire tribe or community', and as such part of that people's inheritance. True to this and surely with personal implications he endorses Thomas Mann's view of art as somehow 'anonymous and communal'.

But his observations could also be wryly down-to-earth. In 1967 he was one of three writers brought to Glasgow for a TV programme in which one of them would be announced the winner of a Scottish Arts Council prize. On the Saturday night the BBC put him up in a glass and plastic monstrosity of a hotel near Kelvingrove. Next morning I went to collect him, to take him home for a bite to eat. He appeared in the foyer in a polo-necked sweater, and suggested we have a drink. As neither of us was wearing a tie we were not allowed into the fuggy lounge – but had to stand in the doorway, sipping our begrudged half-pints. After lunch I delivered him to Broadcasting House, wished him luck and said goodbye.

Several days later a card came from Orkney. In it George remarked dryly that he'd been taken back to the hotel late that evening. As he clambered out of his taxi, 'they were shovelling the drunks into the gutter . . . *all wearing ties'.* He had in fact won the award: now, he said, he was glad to be settling back to his interrupted work schedule.

Years later another letter from Orkney hinted at the rigour of custom: dated 31 December it ended, 'I must go now. I hear them coming for me.' This evoked dim memories of the Abbotsford, Milne's and Paddy's Bar. But he belonged to and was identified above all with his own environment: the world of almost treeless landscapes and stark seascapes he transformed for his readers, and where he preferred to remain a 'word-voyager [who] rarely voyages far from his rocking-chair'. Even a travel bursary lured him no further than Dublin. And latterly he was deprived of choice by illness: those prolonged stays in hospital which made him, as he graphically put it, 'trenched by wounds', alternating with periods of painful recuperation at home.

Gunnie Moberg once persuaded him to travel as far as Oxford – their train-journey a saga in itself. But his dislike of travel was well documented. It may even have entered the realm of folk-legend: as recently as last autumn arrivals for the launch in Edinburgh of a book about his work were startled to hear the event had been called off because the author (George's face beaming from the cover was indicated) hadn't managed to get down for the occasion.

A striking aspect of George's poetry is how right from the outset he homed in on themes which were to prove constant preoccupations throughout his life. 'Prayer to Magnus', his first poem in the *New Shetlander* (October, 1947) invoked Magnus as hero and saint, and icon of an age from which our own was seen as an indictable regression. There were echoes of Dylan Thomas and Yeats; with Hopkins an early and lingering love. But he soon found an individual voice, attuned to his subject-matter. With his conversion to Catholicism came a consolidation of Christian ritual and symbol, often in incantatory form. At the same time (and especially in the authorial voice prevalent in his masterly stories) I sensed something of a residual Calvinism on the cusp of his Catholicism. And alongside his hierarchy of creatures with Christ at its summit, his work embraced images of the paganism so dominant in Orkney's Viking inheritance.

His work is peopled by legendary figures to whom he gives social immediacy, and by real people whom he presents as the stuff of legend: Thorfinn, Halcro, Arnor, Flett, Mansie, Janet and Jeems; the tinkers and farmers, mermaids and fishermen and selkie-folk of the north. They recur, as vivid and alive as today's equivalents. At times his handling of them may appear over-exotic, or their two-dimensionality skirt naivety. Predominantly though, in the way they tap his instinctive sources and affections, and eulogise and elegise the immemorial use of land and sea, they convey a sense of being 'precious secrets handed down from generation to generation'.

There are direct links with those Norsemen who in 1153 rifled Maeshowe, carving in the stone their stick-figure-like runes: an eerily torchlit reminder of the mediaeval warring of beauty and decay; the fate of those who during their lives helped fill the world with colour and splendour, and the *danse macabre* which catches up all trades and ages.

As the years went by and to my regret, I saw George less and less. But through his letters I remained conscious from afar – as did the multitude of friends to whom he wrote, in his inimitable roundhand – of his humanity and humility, his gritty integrity and ready encouragement of others. In conjunction with this, and the intensity of his vision and determination to 'keep the sources pure', I marvel at his gift for rendering language simultaneously (and inimitably) his own, yet a mouthpiece for his Islands and (as he saw them) their people.

Socially and despite his shyness, he seemed to put at ease those who might otherwise have remained awkward in one another's company. Here man and poet were one: nothing and no one, however nominally lowly, lacking significance or uniqueness in the scheme of things. Nor did he evade the extremes of the human condition: on the one hand *'A silent conquering army, / The island dead, / Column on column, each with a stone banner / Raised over his head.'* ('Kirkyard'); on the other a trust, at the last, in love's redemptive power. Latterly he seems not only to have achieved a harmony between those inseparables, his life and his life's work; but with a peace of mind tempered by fortitude, to have acknowledged their imminent completion. Integral too, throughout his span as a writer, were his Music and his concept of the Muse.

His early poetry has many musical references: from 'The Old Women' who, gloating over a drowned fisher-boy, *'weave into their moans / an undersong of terrible holy joy'*, to the red poet Arnor decreeing: *'Drop my harp / Through a green wave, off Yesnebay, / The next time you row to the lobsters'* ('The Five Voyages of Arnor'), and the brothers of Eynhallow singing *'Star of the Sea, shine for us'* ('Our Lady of the Waves').

Then his stories. From his first volumes *A Calendar of Love* and *A Time to Keep* they have a rich poetic charge: the controlled flow and textures of the prose drawing on his poet's crafting of verse-forms, a familiarity with the art and discipline of shaping and compressing. Often structured (like so many of his poems) in keeping with the Seasons or what he saw as the mysterious figure seven, theirs is a compact mesh of assonance and alliteration, satisfying to ear and eye. Underlying their burnished natural descriptions is the rhythmic pulse of his music.

His forays into dramatic form are also reverberant. Chronicling the centuries *A Spell for Green Corn* is dominated by the blind fiddler Storm Kolson, his instrument the one favoured by the islanders of Hellya. The play's last line reads 'Here then is the music for controlling the machines.' *The Voyage of St Brandon* opens with an old man carrying a battered harp along a road, has in it birds that sing Matins, and ends: 'Blessed be the Word. Amen.'

In his various genres, thematic threads can be traced. In the poem-sequence *Fishermen with Ploughs*, folk fleeing pestilence founded an agricultural community in Rackwick. Centuries later comes devastation by a hideous Black Flame. Between lies the cycle not just of the seasons but the birth and death of a civilisation. It is no longer merely the machines that are evil, but their appalling manifestation in the Bomb. His first novel *Greenvoe* depicts five typical days in the life of a remote Island village. Caught in a nightmare of destruction it succumbs to the (unspecifed) threat of 'Black Star'. His last novel *Beside the Ocean of Time*, written twenty-two years later, again depicts the destruction of an Island community and its way of life – this time through preparations for War. The title is worth a passing thought.

In his autobiographical *For the Islands I Sing* George recalls deriving 'days of intense delight' from Thomas Mann's *The Magic Mountain.* Set as it is in a sanatorium for victims of consumption, the illness for which he had already been hospitalised, it is no surprise that book made a deep impression on him. One chapter in Mann's novel opens by suggesting a resemblance between the medium of narration and that of music, in the way both fill up time. That chapter, intriguingly, is called *By the Ocean of Time.*

In George's own book the central character is Thorfinn, whose vivid 'daydreams' as a boy are set against the struggle of his adult writer self, desperately seeking inspiration. In the chapter 'The Muse' the boy encounters a girl on horse-back, gold hair streaming. To him she is Persephone – her horse Pegasus, the winged steed caught by Perseus as it drinks at what Keats called 'the pure, the blissful Hippocrene'. The birds here though are skylarks, not nightingales. Sophie leaves, but in due course her older self will rejoin him, on his return to the desecrated island. She brings sustenance – and the prophecy 'It is our son who will be the poet'. She is unambiguously Thorfinn's Muse. But not exclusively his: she will help to engender a next generation. Her role – the regeneration of language – is to be a continuing one; the note of affirmation she strikes hinting at a continuity, beyond him.

A direct line can be drawn between this pivotal figure and someone to whom George was close, and for whom he retained a lasting fondness. In *For the Islands I Sing* he writes: 'The idea of the Muse who brings out the best in artists is ancient, of course. Some modern poets have their Muse, a woman who transfigures their work and guides them like a star, *stella maris.* This girl was actually called Stella.' And of her death: 'Somewhere in the great music, she is lost.' Much has been said and written, not least by George himself, on Stella Cartwright's closeness to him. Rather than pursue this I'd like to posit, alongside the continuing presence (albeit in absence) of that real-life 'star of the sea', another – prior – source of 'inspiration'.

Earlier he speaks of the legendary and historical events, and their 'violent beauty', which were to provide a vivid backdrop for so much of his writing. Had it not been for these, he tells us, 'the talent that will not let one rest would have had to latch on to other themes'. This draws us fascinatingly towards an intimate source of his voice as a writer, which preceded any other – because it was in his bloodstream.

Joseph Brodsky suggests in a stimulating essay that a vital role in a poet's early development might be played by 'the Muse, née language'. This certainly seems the case with another writer whose preference was for the humble life: the Icelander Halldor Laxness. Not only does Laxness's prose reflect the understated and at times almost cinematic technique of the Sagas: in his novel *The Happy Warriors* he attacks the evils of totalitarianism and the submissiveness of artists and intellectuals to despots. In his 1955 Nobel laureate acceptance speech Laxness made a point of paying tribute to his family, and especially his grandmother who taught him 'hundreds of lines of old Icelandic poetry before [he] ever learned the alphabet'.

I don't know that George went quite that far. But while doubting whether he could have written 'at a time, 150 years ago, when life was dangerous and the language rich, and the community invested with a kind of ceremony; [and] the people lived close to the springs of poetry and drama, and were not aware of it', he specifically states: 'I draw any art I have from great-grandparents, and further back; I acknowledge the gift and the debt, but I would not have wished to live their hard lives.'

He acknowledged his bardic role as a repository for familial and tribal voices, one a conduit for the other. This identification of the *'Muse'* was to him not airy-fairy but very real. He also sensed a cultural dichotomy. *For the Islands I Sing* acknowledges the provenance of the pared-down style that was his hallmark: 'The structure and form of the saga stories are magnificent. I think I have learned from them the importance of pure shape.' He then pinpoints another quality and its source: 'But from my mother's side, the Celtic, I delight too in decoration. Whether it is desirable to marry 'pure narrative' with elaborate decoration is not for me to say. I write as I must.'

This offers a revealing insight into an uncompromising temperament. The 'delight' inherited from his mother, a Gaelic-speaker from Strathy in Sutherland, is nowhere more evident than in the grace and intricacy of those poems (with none of the self-pastiche that sometimes infiltrated his work) inspired during his last illness, by Gunnie Moberg's haunting Orkney photographs with their at times almost abstract beauty. 'Swans' from *Orkney Pictures and Poems*, the Colin Baxter book on which they collaborated, ends: *'Their blue and silver palace a prison, / They walk on the ice of exile, those princesses'*.

Language can be seen as a dual inspiration: drawn in or inhaled literally at his mother's knee, then in turn breathed into his writing. Not simply absorbed and passed on but added to, and enhanced. Imagine with each generation words passing through an hour-glass, in this instance to be not just preserved but transformed. So that he didn't merely contribute to the language but as Seamus Heaney resonantly put it, 'turned into part of the language, a language changed by what he recalled to it, and bequeathed to it anew'.

A recurring motif throughout his work is that of the well: from the reputed healing powers of the waters by the road-side near Brinkie's Brae to the turgid sweetness of the condemned well facing 'the day of the long lead pipe'; from his play of that name ending with fragments of flute song and the Keeper of the Well welcoming voyagers, to this short poem quoted in the programme for his 70th birthday celebration in Edinburgh's Queen's Hall:

A Work for Poets

To have carved on the days of our vanity
A sun
A ship
A star
A cornstalk

Also a few marks
From an ancient forgotten time
A child may read

That not far from the stone
A well
Might open for wayfarers

Here is a work for poets –
Carve the runes
Then be content with silence.

Fittingly, George chose this to be the last poem in his posthumous collection *Following a Lark*. It indeed reads like an epitaph – but a hortatory one. His task done, the runes carved (but with a simplicity a child may read), the poet (or his inheritor?) is to be 'content with silence'. But it is the silence of the well: not simply a place of darkness and resonance; but a symbol of refreshment and sustenance. W.B. Yeats, no stranger to the plucking of the harp, ended up in 'shadowy waters'. Even Norman MacCaig, more prolific than most, finally conceded, 'the well is dry'. The marvel is that for George, the well never seemed to dry. But that with the single-mindedness of the true artist, and no little indomitability of body and spirit, he should have remained responsive to the impulse within him. And the world immediately around him.

ORKNEY SHORE

A cormorant flew
round the Peerie Sea
as if to say:
this belongs to me.

But the island mists
grew grey then white,
till the island rose
on a ribbon of light.

The hourglass island
webbed him in
with the scything wings
of his own dark sin.

The treeless land
may break back, but he
will be shell and skull
in the Peerie Sea.

WINTER

Part of the Bay seemed to freeze.
Between here and the Point
was suspended a curtain
of spray, a frill of silk.

Birds wintered here, blown
off course. A spoonbill,
taken on one of the skerries,
was sent to the museum –

its breast shot away. 'Worst
since '41 when two smacks
had their keels crushed and the Tink
was found, hands stuck

to a metal drum.' I concede
things were worse in those days.
Nevertheless I take
what they say with a pinch

of salt, knowing how in time
I shall describe this
Winter's glory: ice to the Kame,
the seals surfacing with ruffs of lace.

A Human Trembling

IAIN CRICHTON SMITH

Although already an avid admirer of Iain Crichton Smith's poetry, it was with his first hardback *Thistles and Roses* in 1961 that I really fell under his spell: its crystalline forms and honeyed cadences, its evidence of an enquiring mind and sense of moral order. The flyleaf indicated unambiguously that 'he was born in 1928 in Lewis, Outer Hebrides'. And the title reflected what so preoccupied him: the conflict between discipline and freedom, between the thorniness of the island he had grown up in and the achieved perfection of art. His next collection *The Law and the Grace*, the title more theologised, its imagery as startling but more austere, depicted dogma in combat with what he saw as some kind of 'unpredictable energy' – or by analogy, poetic inspiration grappling with the control of the metre.

For a while we corresponded, and I saw many of his poems before they appeared in print. In 1966 I'd broadcast his verse dialogue 'Columba and Knox' (along with 'Ikey the Tinker' by George Mackay Brown and an Edwin Morgan duologue between Hieronymus Bosch and Johann Faust). Then while I was holidaying on Loch Awe he suggested I visit him in Oban. On my arrival he left me with his mother and went for groceries. During our conversation she spoke of the past and of her return to Lewis. I nodded: 'Ah, that'd be when Iain was born.' 'No,' she said, 'Iain was born

in Glasgow.' Just then he returned and whisked me away. In later biog.
notes, despite what his mother had said and the internal evidence of the
poems ('*I left you, Glasgow, at the age of two / and so you are my birthplace
just the same*') he tended to retain Lewis, I suspect either through an
unwillingness to align himself with a city he regarded as alien, or from an
inner urge for consistency between his purported birth*place* and his
birth*right*.

At the age of seventeen he had left the island for the first time to go to
University in Aberdeen. He has described how on emerging from the
railway station there, the sight of a beggar with a cap beside him on the
pavement made a big impact on him. Across the street from his student
lodgings was a statue of Byron. Very soon Lewis would seem 'a world away
both in space and in time'. In later life certainly he could not contemplate
returning there to live. Yet he always perceived himself as an islander, much
of his writing over the years reverting to an island setting and psychological
milieu. Looking back he claimed Lewis had given him 'images of the sea,
and the bare mind'.

One image which recurs almost compulsively is that of the Old Woman
figure, bowed with age and portrayed with varying degrees of pity and
helplessness, from his early (and perhaps most anthologised) '*And she, being
old, fed from a mashed plate . . .*' to the existential desperation of

> *O dear God*
> *wherever you are, I am almost driven wild*
> *by your frightening flowers whose blossoms are turned to bone*
> *for an old woman to look at in a small room alone.*

> — 'OLD WOMAN WITH FLOWERS' —

Elsewhere, with her set mouth, neither she nor her narrow theology escapes
rigorous scrutiny:

> *Your thorned back*
> *heavily under the creel*
> *you steadily stamped the rising daffodil.*

> — 'OLD WOMAN' —

As his poems shed their early lushness, so the short plays he embarked on proved even more stark in their often surreal probing of states of mind. Many of their themes can be traced to earlier sources in his poems and stories, as a river might tap underground springs or be fed by a runnel-work of tributaries. And though the full-length stage plays came considerably later, he had long shown an interest in writing in dramatic form. Shortly after we first met he wrote me:

> I've been playing around recently. I've written a play rather like a Round the Horn script set in a girls boarding school. I was thinking I might give it to the school and someone might put it on. But I'm rather doubtful. I wrote it all in one night throwing in everything that came into my head. The matron turns out to be a Russian spy, etc., etc.

I've no idea whether that one saw the light of day. A host of others certainly did – many, written for radio, remaining unpublished. These were remarkable not for their complex sound effects or concern with technical innovation but for their trust in the *language*, their economy and sensitivity to speech nuances and an ability to map the unease lurking beneath what was said. They also seem to bear out his view of himself as a writer for whom 'writing comes not from width of experience but obsessions'.

In his collection of essays *Towards the Human* he says, 'I am not writing for anyone in particular. I am writing to a secret command, in answer to the sudden flash of an image from a street, from a record, from a wood.' Elsewhere he wonders whether Scottish poets (himself included), though good at landscape, are not so hot at 'plotting the quick movements of the living being'. Precisely this quality informs his plays.

By the Sea, in which an elderly couple meet on the front at Helensburgh, is a touching study of loneliness in old age, framed by fairground music rising and falling on the breeze. Years later in his last play *On the Bench*, the man and woman are joined by two peripheral characters. But right from its down-to-earth opening the tone and tempo are very different: it is inventively entertaining in its own right, not merely a recycling of the original.

The characters in *On the Bus* are soured by petty snobberies and the routine trivia of their lives. In *The Smile* (which quarries the short story *A Night with Kant* – or vice versa) the strolling philosopher is bemused by his town's demi-monde; while *The Visitor* (from a story called *Mr Heine* and later a stage play) is an indictment of bourgeois complacency and intolerence. *The Voices* opens on Christmas morning: a man hears an echoing cry from space, saying 'L o v e'. When he records this and plays the machine back, there is nothing there. Helpless, he howls like a wolf.

Part of the excitement of directing his work was its unpredictability. Out of the blue one day came a script called *Goodman and Death Mahoney*, a witty pastiche western written in verse and narrated by a tobacco-spittin' old cow-puncher. Set to jaunty music by Robert Pettigrew it was heard first on Radio Scotland, then (to the bemusement of some of the more po-faced members of programme review board in London) on Radio 3.

Columcille, staged in 1997 to mark the 1400th anniversary of Columba's death, was memorable for its telling simplicity of image and the conversations between the ageing Saint and his younger self – played with utter conviction, not by a boy but by an actress. This Columba was human and humane, with no high-flown rhetoric, no tortuous theologising or attacks on dogma.

Lazy Bed, his second full-length piece in English, was built round its central character Murdo's refusal to get out of bed and his combat with the figure of Death, black-clad and carrying a scythe. Certain incidents in this wonderfully idiosyncratic take on the *Oblomov* story were, as Iain put it in the programme, 'based on real-life happenings'. He then added, with delicious understatement, 'The mother-son relationship has also interested me.'

One motif from his poetry which appears in the play is a blue vase belonging to Murdo's mother and purloined after her death by a neighbour – only for his girlfriend to get it back. Here the vase, the blue of the sky and with its classic overtones, is a symbol of order, of timeless perfection. Not unlinked to the radiance of love – and its awakening in Murdo:

> How can I prove my love and will Judith love me back? She seems so self-confident, so complete in herself. Last night I dreamed of her. I dreamed I was putting slates on the roof and writing on them at the same time. Now that my mother is dead I am permitted to love. Is that not the answer to the riddle?

Iain loved the magic of the theatre. I remember particularly our going, one Edinburgh Festival, to see the Rustavelli Company's *Richard III*. I'll never forget the power of the acting, the dark imagery and sense of danger – or his scarcely containable elation in the foyer afterwards.

His prodigality regarding his own work was common knowledge. When I rang to check the text of a sequence of autumn poems it turned out he hadn't kept a copy. Sounded on punctuation he'd say, 'Oh, just use whichever you think best.' His typewriter ribbon was so frayed that if you turned the envelope with the script in it upside-down, the middle of his 'o's and 'b's and 'd's fell out like confetti. The bottom lines tended to undulate. And he didn't hyphenate 'no one', so his plays were peppered with references to this mysterious character *Noone*.

In the studio as elsewhere his hilarity and puckishness were infectious. His giggle must still ring in the ears of everyone who knew him. In one of the first poetry readings I did with him, in Stirling, he solemnly introduced the intriguingly eclectic *White Air of March* as from his 'Eliot phase'. A few lines in he doubled up and spluttered: 'Of course I meant George, not T.S.' Once we'd the daft notion of him being interviewed in a rowing-boat, with Loch Etive gently lapping. Only to find the tape-machine batteries were flat. We went to get new ones. Then it turned out the microphone-cable had snapped. By the time the local blacksmith had soldered it and we had been suitably refreshed, the tide had gone out. We set up anyway. But by now the midges were out in droves. Needless to say Iain's giggle had become a cosmic chortle.

In the early days Iain might stay with my wife Judy and myself in Glasgow or else book into a nearby hotel – and we'd walk back late to the bleak room and dim light-bulb that would feature in his stories. Little doubting the pressures on him of Art and Life: the one redefining the other. About one thing he was, even then, emphatic:

> No poetry which does not deal with human beings can in the end be worth much. Nature is all right, but we aren't hills or rivers or haystacks. Even Stevens is at his best only when dealing with human beings. I sensed this truth intuitively many years ago: now I'm utterly convinced of it. Philosophy, politics, scenery, etc., are not important in comparison with the pathos of the human being.

He could for all that be ill at ease in his human contacts. Visiting us, he seemed loath initially to meet Judy's eye; referring to her even in her presence as *she*, as if bound by some social hesitancy or inhibition. Beside me as I write are two photographs: one a carefree figure, with eager eyes and laughter-crinkles; the other domed and spectral, under the burden of the years. Both are of Iain. The latter though, is by far the earlier – the other his later self.

The death in 1969 of his mother whom he'd looked after for seven years left him 'aimless and rudderless'. Yet he was becoming ever more prolific. Once I bumped into Norman MacCaig in Edinburgh's George Street: he said he was really worried about Iain, adding sternly: 'He hasn't had a book out for days.' But though Iain applied the word 'spontaneous' to himself he made clear his belief that 'great poetry' should be intellectually founded. Nor was he driven as some writers are merely by a compulsion to fill the page, but by an implacable moral imperative.

A man as well as a poet of bewildering dichotomies, he could veer from childlike curiosity to profundity, from hilarity to black despair. For all his mercurial wit and atrocious puns there remained dark undercurrents and a dread of the mind's domination by spurious authority figures: 'any form of ideology'. Detestation of dogma pulses through his work, with at the heart of it a deep resentment at the Church's hold over his mother. On the publication of his 1970 *Selected Poems* he revealingly wrote me:

> All my poetry springs from a rebellion against the darkness
> and dimness of my upbringing . . . all trying to prove to the
> old lady she was wrong.

Two years previously he had channelled this, and a passionate resentment at the cruelty of the Clearances and the 'hobnailed mind' of the perpetrators, into his first novel *Consider the Lilies*. Written at white heat and with its penetrating insight into the mind of old Mrs Scott, it had been read on radio, and praised, even prior to its publication. Yet when it appeared he confided:

> The more I see it, the more I realise I ought never to have
> published it. I have of course been reading Russian novels, but
> even without them I should have realised it's a lot of
> tripe . . . It's what I would call Turgenev-and-water.

The reviews (their concern at anachronisms aside) and the instant acclaim with which the book was received would vehemently dispute this. But it pained me to see someone whose work was of such quality, and who was held in such esteem and affection, so persistently bludgeoned by self-doubt. Matching this were the self-effacing inscriptions in the gift-copies of his novels and stories. But not, interestingly enough, where the poetry was concerned.

When public readings became the rage, he initially expressed a dislike for them – then took to them like a duck to water and to the delight of a widening circle of admirers, spanning all age-groups. There were fellowships, to Australia and Canada. While easing financial pressures after he gave up teaching, it all added to the burden on him. Yet he couldn't have been more generous of his time and energy, on committees or in encouraging younger writers. Or more courteous and modest in receipt of his many accolades and honours: from an Aberdeen University doctorate and the Saltire Book of the Year Award, to PEN's silver pen (which he later sheepishly said he thought he'd lost) and the OBE.

To everyone who knew them, Iain's marriage to Donalda was the most marvellously warming and transforming thing that could have happened to him. In due course came the move to Taynuilt. But complex forces were to take over, not least through the distance he now was from the sea. His favourite song, along with *An Ealla Bhàn (The White Swan)*, was *An Atarachd Ard (The High Wave)*, in which an old man asks to be buried within the sound of the ocean. Eventually came the breakdown, on which he drew later with startling honesty and lucidity in his novel *In the Middle of the Wood*.

These were terrifying times for himself and Donalda – and the way she saw him through was to be marvelled at. One outcome was that where previously Iain had felt it enough simply to examine life, he now needed to find a *freedom* in poetry: 'a freedom operating in the human mind'. *The Human Face*, his book-length sequence written in the Burns stanza, he described as 'a torch for humanism, sometimes trembling but sincere'. In a radio feature he analysed and acknowledged this new liberation with typical objectivity:

> Yes, I am much less exiled from myself, and also from other people. I think the two are interdependent. If you're exiled from other people you tend also to be exiled from yourself. I think it was Thom Gunn who spoke about 'the dark world in which we walk with everyone'. We must try to live with each other, and not impose our systems on anybody. That's what I've learned, that people ought to be respected because they're human. That's what it's all about, really.

His poetry continued to display those uncanny leaps of the intuition, those exuberant short-circuitings of logic, unique to him. I've heard them attributed to English being a second tongue: a contributing factor maybe, but surely far from the whole story. As for word-associations: where these come into play, their impact is often heightened by the range of knowledge and cultural reference at his disposal. The 'leaps' which might appear to parallel the natural *joie-de-vivre* and spontaneity of his 'two girls singing' in the poem of that name are nowhere more breathtaking than in the one which starts '*Listen, I have flown through darkness towards joy*', and ends uncannily with the grooved armour of statues rising and walking away

> *into a resurrection of dead villages,*
> *townspeople, citizens, dead exiles,*
> *who sing with the salt in their mouths,*
> *winged nightingales of brine.*

> – 'Listen' –

This is his brand of the 'hallucinatory quality' he'd admired in MacDiarmid's early work, of which in *The Golden Lyric* he wrote: 'Whatever the imagination is, there is no doubt it is what we require in poetry at the highest level. How it operates is incomprehensible.' For all its vision and sustained meditation, he saw his own 'Deer on the High Hills' as 'not the outcome of conscious, philosophic thinking, or a blue-print – I don't know where it came from'. The same letter describes his rushing home to get 'By Ferry to the Island' down before he lost it . . . 'like carrying water home in a bucket'. Robert Frost said: 'Like a piece of ice on a hot stove, the poem must ride on its own melting.' At times Iain's seemed scarcely given a chance to melt.

Then of course there was the anarchic philosopher-joker Murdo. His first public appearance was in a novella-length story in 1981, his zany world between that of a child's day-dreams ('a lavatory made of diamonds') and nightmares ('a witch with her cup of blood'); shouting to the stars and asking his local librarian for *War and Peace* by Hugh MacLeod. His accumulated *Thoughts* followed, and at readings reduced audiences to helplessness. By a fascinating process of osmosis and by way of *Lazy Bed*, Murdo finally became the persona for Iain's own autobiography, a distancing device enabling him 'to make comedy of painful experience'. It contains a hilarious indictment of the absurdity of National Service, and a painfully funny cameo on B & B's. It is very affecting on the poverty of his early upbringing and his solitary yearnings. He unblinkingly acknowledges his guilt towards his mother; and what marriage to Donalda so richly meant to him. There is an affectionate section on their visit to his Uncle Torquil, in Canada. Yet constantly signalled are the fierce divisions within him. And time and again he disarmingly skates over what seems life's futility with a coruscating wit, wisdom and wordplay which render things palatable: like a string of fairy-lights stretched across an abyss.

Years before, in a review of W.S. Graham's *Collected Poems*, Iain had written that the 'real poem' could be 'the *dark companion* travelling alongside the one actually created'. I've known no writer more at the mercy of the circling fins of his own 'dark companions' or so triumphant in his retrieval of underwater treasure, often from dark and swirling depths. In the wake of and despite his breakdown he felt much more affirmative, more appreciative of 'where I live now, a natural world of great beauty'. This had an impact on what he wrote subsequently. Alasdair Maclean, drawing his inspiration from stony Ardnamurchan, believed 'death was the noblest and most profound of the great themes of poetry, or what the love poets turn to when they put away childish things'. Iain Crichton Smith reiterated that the two need not be mutually exclusive, most poignantly in *The Leaf and the Marble*, an extended love poem published shortly after his death in the autumn of 1998.

Drawing on an illustration of Tutankhamun's golden throne with the 19-year-old king and his wife in profile – he seated, she standing, their eyes level – the exquisitely-wrought sequence starts with a holiday in Italy then with a vibrancy of classical allusion contrasts the world of nature and the world of man, the transient and the eternal, the *leaf* and the *marble*. It then becomes a meditation on the fond gaze between the royal pair – with love 'the chain / that lightly binds them together / in this airy blue'.

> *How tiny the leaf*
> *against the shadow of Rome, of*
> *ideology. And yet*
> *how precious, I touch it*
> *and it burns my hand . . .*

My leaf,
my sail, mark of the present,
transitory coming and going, badge
of the present.
        Love, my love,
leaf shining so greenly
against the green-eyed wolf.

One line in particular strikes to the heart: '*When everything trembles, only love holds it together.*' With this as a motif the poem as a whole is not simply a distillation of wisdom and intuition but a revelation of Iain's inner nature and values – aesthetically and within marriage. The dedication 'for Donalda with love and gratitude' speaks for itself.

Malcolm's Land

W.S. GRAHAM

Not so long ago I was sent an issue of a poetry magazine devoted to 'the South West of England', which the editorial defined as incorporating 'the urban, the pastoral and the experimental *as no other area*' (my italics). Doubtless the region's literary output reflects these – and the Celtic spirit of Cornwall. I wondered if the claim to uniqueness stemmed from a use of language, specifically Cornish, not evident in the issue in question. Otherwise the claim is surely equivocal.

Many a catchment area must be inhabited by writers with an ear to the ground, urban and rural (not to mention litoral), determined to 'make it new'. Scotland with its triple linguistic inheritance of English, Scots and Gaelic would more emphatically seem to meet the requirement of 'as no other area'. Many of its current manifestations might arguably be considered unique. Even then I'd be hesitant to trumpet them as such: preferring to think not of any specific or received new mode, but of there being as many around as one cares to imagine. Nor need one approach, however fashionable or *outré*, invalidate others.

I prefer to believe it's through an alert sensibility and original way of seeing, and an ear attuned to living speech patterns, rather than any gratuitous ventriloquism or acrobatics, that a writer can best reflect a specific locale, yet be universal. All of which strike me as epitomised by a poet I have long regarded with a warmth disproportionate to any closeness between us comparable to that of many other writers I've come to know and admire – and think of as friends.

W.S. Graham was born in Greenock, Renfrewshire, in 1918. In 1938 he was awarded a bursary to the residential Adult Education College of Newbattle Abbey. One of his fellow-students was Nessie Dunsmuir, whom he was later to marry. The following year Graham went to work in Eire, before returning to Clydeside where he had a spell as a precision-engineer in a torpedo factory. Also in Glasgow at this time was C.M. Grieve (Hugh MacDiarmid), whose advocacy of a complete regeneration not only of Scottish literature, but in all walks of Scottish life, laid the foundation for the self-styled modern Scottish Renaissance.

Rather than be part of this and with an apocalyptic first volume *Cage Without Grievance* (Parton Press, 1944) already under his belt, Graham headed south – at the same time as the painters Colquhoun and MacBryde. Already he saw himself as 'banished, more or less, from the Scottish lit. scene, which I don't hold with and seems to get more embarrassing with its playing bards and glimmerin lufts keekin wi sna'. In 1947 he won an Atlantic Award for poetry, and in 1947–48 lectured at New York University. But home, for virtually the rest of his life, would be Madron, in Cornwall; among his companions the artists Peter Lanyon, Roger Hilton and Bryan Wynter. Each in his medium, pursuing modes of experimentation and abstraction.

His progress from his first Faber volume *The White Threshold* (1949) by way of the verbal exuberance and rhythmic muscularity of *The Nightfishing* (1955) to the maturity of *Malcolm Mooney's Land* (1970) and *Implements in their Places* (1977) represents (though he'd defend his early work, disputing implications of a neat 'progress') a striking voice-change. It is easy to see his confrontation with the ice-bound abyss and the frontiers of the imagination, as contemporaneous with Beckett. Neither evades his sense of mortality, of bleakness. Graham too could walk the tightrope between rigorous depiction of the human predicament, and a linguistic friskiness and sense of fun. Allied to his mastery of form and furtherance of poetic technique, this makes it the more regrettable that since his death in 1986 he has on both sides of the Atlantic been if far from unrecognised, in my view sadly and mistakenly undersung.

The first of my sporadic and brief contacts with him was asking him to go to his local BBC studio, to record two poems. When I telephoned the office there to see if someone would look after a poet for me, there was a female shriek at the other end. 'Not Mister Graham? The one who wants whisky with his boiled eggs, for breakfast!' The only time I went to hear him read in the flesh, he gave the impression of boiled eggs aplenty. Rocking slowly on his heels, he kept asking those in the audience who loved him to put their hands up. I found it an oddly discomfiting gesture of insecurity in so handsome and ebullient a figure. He got through the evening. But a recording I'd intended afterwards had to be abandoned.

Introducing a selection of his poems on radio he described one as 'narrow on the page', then invited listeners to envisage it surrounded by whiteness: a whiteness simultaneously linking yet isolating poet and listener. As he put it in a *Poetry Society Bulletin*: 'I am always very aware that my poem is not a telephone call. The poet only speaks one way. He hears nothing back. His words as he utters them are not conditioned by a real ear replying from the other side.'

A wider *whiteness* was both a source and a setting for a dominant area of his output. Those sequences set in a metaphoric Malcolm Mooney's Land, an arctic of the mind, deal with the dilemma and desperation of communication – and non-communication. I find it no surprise that one of Graham's foremost admirers was Harold Pinter. His white expanses could be icily cerebral. At other times his was an intractably literal (as against purely literary) floe. And in his maraudings he was equally a voyager of the imagination, of language and its originality.

Even then he could be demanding. This may be why he remains, as I say, one of the most seriously under-regarded, and critically neglected, of contemporary poets. Indeed a reason for his springing particularly to my mind of late is that on being sounded on the contents-list for a proposed (and very comprehensive) anthology of Scottish poetry, and asked to comment on any absentees or deserving candidates, I preferred first to focus on what struck me as Graham's under-representation. Not least because it was his other, more intimate side which was absent.

This and his music, especially when he slips into Scottish idiom and cadences, make him for me one of the most touching of poets. As in the simplicity of 'To Alexander Graham' with its retrospective realisation that he must have loved his late father; and the elemental quality of his love-lyrics to his wife. Indeed it is to Nessie that many of his most delicate and at the same time vulnerable poems are addressed; at times with the eerie simplicity of a ballad, or children's rhyme. The last poem in his *Collected Poems 1942–1977* (Faber, 1979) – on the dust-jacket of which he insisted on being described as 'a Greenock man' – ends:

Nessie Dunsmuir, I say
Wheesht wheesht to myself
To help me now to go

Under into somewhere
In the redcoat rain.
Buckle me for the war.

Are you to say goodnight
And kiss me and fasten
My drowsy armour tight?

My dear camp-follower,
Hap the blanket round me
And tuck in a flower.

Maybe from my sleep
In the stoure at Culloden
I'll see you here asleep

In your lonely place.

– 'To my Wife at Midnight' –

A fear of night-beasts is never far away. An ear not attuned to Scots adjustments of rhythm, or subtleties of intonation, may not detect the burden of emotion his words can sustain. But it is at such moments that Graham can make the ground shift from under my feet. The more intense his sense of isolation and desolation, the more aware we are of those emotional nuances, and moments of tenderness, that are among the most private (and precious) links we have.

Each of the few items I retain from him has as it happens a visual impact. One is a postcard with a delicate ink and water-colour by him of pale cliffs and sea. The second seems cut from a piece of card. Its deep blue represents sea and sky. In a garish yellow are a horizon, a star and the outline of a trawler; in white, a hill-line and in block capitals: MALCOLM'S LAND. All might have been drawn hastily by a child. On the reverse: 'Good wishes from W.S. Graham, White Uncle of Malcolm Mooney's Land. 1970–71. Good Hochmagandy.' A third, in its smudged envelope, is a hand-written letter on lined paper, containing a pressed and dried sea-pink.

He journeyed far: not least on the contours of his Don Brown Route, and at the altitudes of Lanyon. He even has a mysteriously Lost Miss Conn, departing from the church fête, leaving the trestle-tables to the wasps. Over the years he crossed many a white threshold. And he never returned from Madron to live in Scotland. For all that and aside from its rhythms so deeply embedded in him, he seems never to have lost an affection for his native land – or to be more accurate, his place of origin: what he termed his 'ark-yard' on the Clyde, Loch Thom with its cackling grouse, or the remembered blue moors of Ayrshire. Part of him appeared to remain haunted by them: as the reader in turn becomes haunted.

One larger-than-life image lingers. A mutual friend visiting Madron vouched for the fact that one night he saw Graham – after a bender – climb unsteadily but determinedly on to the kitchen sink. Feet precariously on the rim, he lurched forward and in the half-dark managed to grab the two taps; then stood joyously imagining he was driving a Glasgow tram.

Another letter to me was recently included in Michael and Margaret Snow's exhilarating and revelatory Carcanet selection of Graham's letters, felicitously entitled *The Nightfisherman*. Dated 27th February '79 it contains a cogent and subjective reason why I have a soft spot for him. In those days he would occasionally enclose a poem. In return I wrote a little one for him. When I sent him it he replied:

> I liked your poem to me. I like your wife even better. (Two different kinds of objects it is true.) Despatch her immediately with soda scones tied in a snow-white towel and a jar of her own make of strawberry jam.

Here as in his poetry I find his voice not diminished or tarnished by the years, but inimitably fresh and captivating.

OWL-WOOD
[FOR JUDY]

We stand at the centre of a perfect hexagon,
the intersections of its swagged segments
so geometric, the squirrels using them
must be accomplished maze-dwellers.

We keep hearing the call of a little-owl
seemingly far away – except we know
it's within a stone's throw: either that
or a figment of the imagination.

Your hand on my arm gives a scarcely
perceptible tremor, as a dusty light-sliver
drifts through sparse willows and settles
to feed its young – mewls faintly audible.

No reason why we shouldn't be here.
For all that, a miraculous affirmation;
as it is that after so many years
there should be such happiness in being together.

Later with you asleep in the car beside me,
ghostly truckloads of logs sucking us into their
slipstream, I think of hunter and haunted –
and an owl's nest, imprinted fluff-balls within.

Horizons
[FOR ARTHUR]

I don't suppose you'll remember
our day by that loch somewhere
up north (I see it but its name has slipped,
over the years, into the shadowy world
between recollection and imagination).

You kept skimming flat stones
on the water, counting how often
they skipped, trying for double
figures. Dreaming really of confounding
the impossible, getting to the other side.

Ever since a matter of smooth stones
gliding across life's perilous
surface. Never again so easy:
aside from wrist or eyesight,
the far shore always further away.

I wish you a strong and accurate
bowling arm, happiness in whatever
you venture. And force not all,
may you find your horizons,
and affections, rewardingly extend.

RESPONSES
[FOR IAN]

Sounds like you're having good times,
though in some ways scarcely
as anticipated: Ayers Rock you say,
a grand climb – if not quite the spiritual
transformation it was cracked up to be.

I envy you the Reef; the thrill
of swimming alongside a sea-turtle,
iridescent fish-shoals in fathoms
clear as crystal: qualities
I seek, in my plunges into poetry –

except more often than not
I surface with little more
than a taste of chlorine
to show for it. No surprise
if you end up the real poet in the family.

Go well meantime, under no such burden;
from pumpkin-picking to playing flanker
for the Burdekin Cane Toads, your own man;
receptive to unknown tunes,
new harmonies: the world your oyster.

Two Summers

Colour postcard of Edinburgh Castle, blossom in foreground:
franked 21 June 1997. In neat round-hand:

Dear Grandma,
Robin and I were really glad to see you yesterday. Just hope our prattling on
didn't tire you. And that you had a good night, with no recurrence of the
pain. We're all packed for our holiday. The strike is off, so no worries on that
score. Bed now, with the alarm set for *de bonne heure pour le départ.* Will
send a card as promised, as soon as we get there. And try to visit all the places
you suggested. Thanks again for everything. Love from us both meantime.
    Fiona.

Sepia postcard of city street, Victorian buildings: dated
Liverpool, 29.5.1915. Black ink, heavy downstrokes.

Dear Louise,
About our journey south and extent of the terrible rail crash near Gretna I
am not at liberty to speak. Though everyone up there will know about it

from the papers. How tragic, before the Royal Scots had even crossed the Channel. Many Watsonians among them. Worsened by the carriage doors being locked. Anyway as a result we have been billeted here. But those that are fit, to be moved on by troopship within a day or so. It cannot come too soon. As we marched along the quay at Lime Street we looked so dishevelled the street-urchins thought we were German prisoners and threw stones at us. Which was hard to bear. No room to say more, except all my love.

And God bless.

Neil.

Colour postcard of Normandy village scene: 24.6.1997.

Dear Grandma,

Robin and I have set foot on French soil for the first time. The sun shining as we drove off the ferry, remembering to keep right. By evening we had reached the little village on the other side of the card, and decided to stay the night. Now we are sitting on a verandah nibbling hot croissants and sipping café au lait. With apple-orchards, as far as the eye can see. Hope all goes well with you.

Love from Robin and me.

Fiona.

Monochrome postcard of nondescript rural scene: heavy franking obliterates place-name: 8.6.1915.

Dear Louise,

I cannot say where we are. Except that it is somewhere in 'la belle France'. And am writing this hastily, for the last post – no pun meant. Had a good journey here. No end to the kindness of the YMCA who had tea waiting at every big station. No saying what lies ahead. But billeted so far in civilian houses. Between you and me, living off the fat of the land. Lewis gun in forenoon, football in afternoon. And confident all will be over soon. Are you still wearing your hair up? I trust this finds you in the pink.

Neil.

Colour reproduction of Renoir's 'Déjeuner des Canotiers':
postmark, Seine 30.6.1997.

Dear Grandma,
Whew! Trust us to reach Paris in a heatwave. Never known it so hot. But exciting. Walked on your beloved *rive gauche.* Unfortunately the trinkets far too dear. Guess where we were yesterday? In the place on the river where Renoir painted his *Luncheon of the Boating Party.* (See over.) The rest'rant re-done up exactly as it was – far smaller than Renoir made it. So many sitters present at one time, an illusion. We did as you said and went down the Champs Élysées to the Arc de Triomphe. Stood ages gazing at the eternal flame marking the last resting-place of France's Unknown Warrior. And thinking of your longlost Neil.
  Much love from Robin and me.
  Fiona.

Featureless monochrome card of landscape with trees:
22.6.1915: postmark illegible.

Dear Louise,
For past weeks, billeted in a barn. Constant torrential rain. Several of our boys laid up with flu. On Saturday rose at 4.30, route march for 21 kilometres. Yesterday attended service of thanksgiving, among the hymns we sang, the 'Auld Hunner'. Increasingly busied by inspections. Now within sound of enemy aircraft. I never was so near God until I came out here. Day and night, He is a comfort. Have been checked for vaccinations, and platoon's precious football put under lock and key: all signs, that we are soon to be on the next stage of our march to Glory!
  God bless.
  N.

Colour card of Fontainebleau Palace, with fountains: written in
pencil: postmark 3.7.1997.

Dear Grandma,
F'bleau outdid expectation. Forests, with huge ants. Formal greenery and
fountains. In the Palace, those endless corridors you spoke of, then the
banquet-hall with its mirrors and crystal chandeliers. Where trumpets
preluded signing the Peace Treaty. Different youth hostels, as we tour
around. Basic, but facilities much improved since your day. Hot water and
all mod cons. I hope you're keeping better.
    Love, R & F. (Forgive pencil, lost pen)

Sepia card of church surrounded by trees: 5.7.1915:
writing blurred as if by rain.

Dear Louise,
Been on Church parade. Imagined I was in the family pew, back home.
Wonder if you are sitting there now. Half hoped for a letter, but was
disappointed. However food parcel arrived, albeit somewhat depleted. For
which real thanks. Have begun to take some extra lodgers on board, which
I could do without. Fortunately we are still at liberty to write letters on
what we are doing. If not our whereabouts, in detail. Orders however to
stand by at an hour's notice. So no saying what lies ahead.
    Your own – Neil.

Colour card of Monet's 'Field with Poppies': date clearly legible,
8.7.1997; but heavily overfranked on picture side. The rounded
writing smaller, hastier.

Hello Grandma!
Hope you like the card. I love the poppies, just splodges of colour close-up.
Have bought a reproduction of it for you. On a little wooden easel. I
thought it might bring back happy memories. Of *la belle France*, as you
always say. It is really good to be away from the city. And heading for
château country. Keep seeing fairy-tale silhouettes on the skyline. Robin

makes up super stories round them, for me. Must hurry to catch the post, or it will have gone.

Love, Fiona.

[A scrawl] And Robin.

[Back to the original writing]

P.S. Whew, mosquitos not as bad as you feared.

Monochrome photograph of do'cots, 12.7.1915: writing more cramped, downstrokes accentuated.

Dear Louise,

Pretty cheerless. Under constant fire from gun batteries and overhead. With nightly sorties. Worst moment, a piece of shrapnel luckily riccochetting off my helmet and another going through my rifle sling. Letter reached me re. Fenwick of 'A' Coy, reported killed a month ago. Replying caused me some thought, as I could not tell the true story of how he met his end. Reported sick with flu, my temp. 99.5°. Driven with 6 others to the C.C.S. but now back down the line. Only regret your parcel not arriving in time. But have left instructions for the others of the platoon to open it.

Your –

Neil.

Colour postcard: aerial view of Château: franked Loire, 12.7.1997: this time, a different and hastier hand:

My turn to write! Never dreamed we'd get so far south. Which was very much thanks to your generous present. Anyway, already almost our last evening. We are spending it in a restaurant, overlooking the milky R. Tarn, with pine-slopes, and precipices, beyond. After an afternoon at a local village fair, where we had our fortune told – in strictest secrecy! Musicians there, in traditional costume, and dancers, and fire-eaters. You would love it. Soon be back home. And can compare notes. Fiona sends love. Me too.

Robin.

*Blank postcard, with address on one side and message on the
other: again heavily franked, date illegible.*

Ma chérie,
You and I will come here, in peacetime again, and sit on the terraces and
sip wine and lie in the hay. Never seen a land so fitted for it. Or swallowtails
the size of here. And fields of fruit, ripe for picking – but bewaring of figs,
now I have learned my lesson (!!). I wish this conflict was over, and long to
be with you again. Because je t'aime beaucoup. And get mad with
frustration and jealousy at the thought of you even meeting other men.
And them meeting your eye. And saying your name. Which is constantly
on my lips . . . At times I fear you are a dream.
    N.

*Colour view of Boulogne harbour: postmark Dover 15.7.1997:
again the rounded writing.*

Dear Grandma,
On board the ferry. The famous White Cliffs in view. (But so far no blue-
birds!) Sorry to hear on phone from Mum about your wee turn. Hope not
too bad. We'll be 2 nights with R's cousin Julie in Lincoln. But look
forward to see you at weekend. Much love meantime. Oh, I wish you
could've seen the bonfires everywhere for the *Quatorze*. Keep smiling.
    Love, Fiona.
    [scrawled below] And Robin.

*A typewritten letter with a field hospital heading, but no specific
name or address: dated 3.9.1915.*

Dear Louise,
I am sorry but do not know how to prepare you. And cannot on my own.
But managed to enlist someone to do so on my behalf. She having
helpfully obliged. The fact is we were instructed to distribute leaflets in
German, urgeing the foe to surrender. We were to wrap these around
stones then after dark head for No Man's Land and throw them towards

the enemy lines. Knowing the consequences but also the penalty for disobeying, we took only a single step from our trench and pushed the stones a little way. Even then many were hit. My legs were blown away. Rendering me a cripple. Along with this, my sight lost. And can thus hold out no hopes of a relationship, other than a perpetual burden. This is to release you, and urge you to pursue your life uncumbered. You must direct your affections elsewhere, dearest. For your future happiness. Forgive me. Do not take this amiss but as it is meant, for the best, I know you have the grit to do so. God bless.

I remain, ever your loving,
Neil.

[Below his signature's downstrokes, and in a spidery blue hand]
As dictated. I am desperately sorry.
Signed, J.Houston [Nursing orderly]

Two Vignettes
SEIGNEUR DE CHERVEUX

My wife and I were on our way to holiday with friends in the south of France. They'd strongly urged us to spend a night in a château they'd been to a couple of times. The proprietor M. Redien had been warmly welcoming. As for his wife's cooking . . .

We'd crossed by overnight car-ferry to Caen and set out before dawn, stopping at Angers to see the Apocalypse tapestries. From there we followed the directions we'd been given. Leaving the main road near Niort we eventually came to the little village of Cherveux (the name of Celtic origin), cut through a farmyard – and there we were. M. Redien, blue eyes darting, led us across the drawbridge into a cool courtyard.

After showing us our room he gave us a tour: first down to the dungeons, then up spiral staircases and along narrow corridors. He proudly pointed out the carvings on the capitals: decorative beasts, and a squatting figure which seemed about to evacuate itself on us. We took in the pantiled roofs and mellow stonework of the donjon opposite; the black-slated turrets above. There was also fine plaster-work, sculpted by Italian craftsmen.

Cherveux was built in the XIIth century on the site of an ancient fortress. But it was when he reached the mid-XVth that M. Redien's eyes really lit up as he spoke a name he'd repeat over and over: Robert du

Cunningham. A favourite of Louis XI, Cunningham was made captain of the king's *garde écossaise*. On the land given him he and his son Joachim built the whole of the present castle in one swoop, incorporating corbels and figures in the Scottish tradition.

No furnishings or portraits remain to conjure up that past. But M. Redien glides vividly down the centuries. The château was occupied by garrisons of swordsmen, only to be confiscated after the Revolution. In 1929 it was declared a historic monument and the following year his parents bought it for the farmland. As its châtelain he thrills to the figure of Cunningham and (unlike the majority of his countrymen, who seem quite unaware of it) delights in the enduring Alliance between France and Scotland.

Supervising the restoration work he dreams that one day the upper floors over the banquet-hall will be rebuilt and that he may live to sleep one night . . . *'juste une nuit'*, in the royal chamber Louis XI occupied while on a pilgrimage. He runs a finger over the coat of arms: two bearded figures bearing a shield bordered by oak-leaves, on it three fleurs-de-lis and a Y-shaped *fourche*. This he assures us commemorates the time Cunningham saved James I of Scotland with a pitch-fork by hiding him under a heap of hay from *'villains Anglois'*.

As the only guests that evening, we ate informally with the family in the vaulted kitchen. From the twirls of Parma ham in melon to the cheeses and fruit M. Redien's fervour for things Scottish increased: James I's poetry, his daughter's marriage to the Dauphin, variants on the name Cunningham.

Our bedchamber with its polished wooden floorboards was over the guardroom. Down several stairs was the bathroom from whose lancet window, cut in the thick walls, you could look out over the moat. During the night I wakened and sensed a presence. Opening my eyes I saw a web of light in the window aperture. Hard to describe, other than that it might have been glancing from a helmet or visor. I couldn't be sure if it was in the room or outside. Slowly it dissolved into the imprint of a man's features. As I screwed my eyes to peer, it faded. Next morning I looked out: the moon would have been far too high, the steadings opposite too low to be a source of light. When we went downstairs the first thing M. Redien asked – the subject had not previously been mentioned – was if we'd seen the *fantôme*. When I gasped he narrowed his eyes, and shrugged: *'ç'est écrit.'* He was delighted we had been visited by the spirited *capitaine*. After breakfast and having paid our bill we said thank-you and goodbye, and he and his wife wished us *bon séjour*.

We were staying near Figeac. Nearby was a richesse of abbeys and châteaux. The tiniest church boasted its misericords. On cycle-runs we'd gawp at portals and cloisters of captivating intricacy. In the face of this the memory of Cherveux and its ghostly Seigneur might have been expected to pall. Instead it proved an ideal springboard. Assier was the strong-hold of the famous braggart Galiot de Genouillac. Rows of wall medallions show him alongside Roman emperors and compare him to Hercules. In the nearby church also built by him, a frieze depicts his exploits. One book on Quercy claims that 'in 1515 he used a new invention, the canon, for the first time': scant consolation to James II, killed when one burst at the Seige of Roxburgh half a century earlier.

As if to counter all this belligerence our guide proves surprisingly *sympathique.* Beckoning us to an alcove she caresses a large framed poster for an exhibition celebrating the 700th anniversary of l'Alliance: a knight on a charger and in crimson and saffron, a sumptuous lion rampant.

High on a cliff overlooking the Lot is the graceful Château de Cénevières, built in the XIIIth century by the lords of Gourdon to spite the English. During the Revolution a mob came to destroy it as a symbol of feudalism. The wily custodian threw open the wine cellars: the château was saved. In a glass case in one room, near a dinner-invitation from Napoleon and documents from Talleyrand, lies a letter from Farnham, Surrey. Dated 1994 it enthuses over the château and gives a promise to return. Then a P.S. '*Le mot d'un écossais est éternel.*' Its signatory Charles Stuart: the current Pretender. Did he also gift the print of a kilted Gordon, to cement a family rapport with the Gourdons?

I warmly recall the feelings we encountered on our trip. As others had previously: among them Scottish guests who promised in the Cherveux visitors' book to try and unearth more about Cunningham. Though I too attempted this, he remains a shadowy figure. But as I picture M. Redien poring over his historical tomes and preserving house-room for his ghostly Seigneur, I wish him good fortune – and the realisation of his dream regarding the royal chamber: '*Mon rêve serait d'y dormir une nuit . . . juste une nuit.*'

Monsieur Bouzou

Marcilhac is on the north bank of the Célé, a tributary of the Lot. Stopping at a roadside auberge and leaving our bicycles in the shade we enjoyed a lunch which began with a rich *terrine du pays* and ended with fruit and coffee. Our objective was the Benedictine abbey. Its Romanesque nave is open to the sky. Only a squat tower stands, its walls overgrown. The Gothic section, rebuilt in the XVth century in flamboyant style, has carved wooden panels, frescoes and coats of arms. In the XIIth century chapter house are sculptured capitals depicting faces with celestial smiles and mythical animals, half monster and half demon, subjecting the lost souls of sinners to appalling punishment.

From a flight of steps overlooking the south portal I became aware of two distinct and separate bursts of activity. In front of me two tourists were taking photographs: not indiscriminately, or casually, but with fixity of intent. The male wore a fore-and-aft cap and despite the warmth, a beige cape. The clickings of his camera were punctuated by lengthy sitings and elaborate refocussings. Intermittently he'd give an elaborate sigh of what seemed aesthetic satisfaction.

His female companion was short and stocky. She had a bigger camera with an electronic zoom-lens. She'd confront each object in a series of feints, like a flyweight boxer; nipping in to catch the unsuspecting stonework unawares, then withdrawing out of arm's reach before the figure on it could retaliate. The only sounds, other than the scliff of shoes on the stone flags of the courtyard, were sharp intakes of breath and a sporadic *'Ja'* or *'Jawohl!'*.

Her rate of strike must have been three times that of her husband round whom she would zigzag dextrously, somehow never clashing with his shutter-movements. As I watched she completed one spool and was on to another; pointing out the base of what to my eye could have been any pillar round any of a hundred now ruined Romanesque abbeys. But they took it from all angles, she finally with knees bent, peering up as though it were the foot of some elephantine creature she was stalking.

At this point I realised I wasn't the only observer. Just inside the portal a small, unkempt figure kept appearing round the wooden half-door. The face seemed undefined, not due to the shadow but because the features were working away, the mouth and eyes never still. The garb might have been that of a monk, or some member of the clergy. Clearly a functionary of the abbey, he seemed to find the antics of the photographers as fascinating as I did. Glancing up he caught my eye and disappeared into the darkness behind the half-door. For a few minutes, nothing. Then he would make tiny forays, flitting out and in like a lizard's tongue so speedily you wondered if you'd seen it at all.

With a last flurry the German couple gathered up their equipment, and went. Instantly the little figure darted gesturing from the doorway. We headed for the portal. Rather than speak he pointed, to the accompaniment of disjointed croaks, at a placard beside the entrance. On it was a speckled newspaper article telling how M. Jean Bouzou was the abbey guide. And as a deaf-mute, communicated with his hands. He pointed at this, at himself – and held out a hand for the requisite 10-francs entry charge. Inside he led us to a side-table on which leaflets were stacked and handed us one in English. He pointed to the numbered paragraphs on the leaflet, indicating in which direction each section lay.

Where he thought we'd missed a significant detail or failed to notice some carved oak-work, he delicately impressed himself upon us. The sounds he made were plaintively disjointed. Then we took in that we were hearing music. An organ was playing. A choir joined in. For a moment we were startled at the thought of our visit coinciding with a mass. Then we realised it was, of course, on tape. To add to the uncanniness, there was no organ in the building. Our guide's duties included switching on and off the ghostly music he could not himself hear. Its reverberant conclusion coincided with the end of our tour. Sensing he was unlikely to pick up any spoken expression of appreciation, I spontaneously clasped his hand, shook it firmly . . . and stepped out into the sun.

We walked alongside the adjacent mill-lade, past clouds of frantically copulating dragonflies. I mused about our little guide, attributing to him both a timeless quality and something I couldn't quite define, but of a period prior to our own. Later, looking up from unpadlocking our bicycles, I noticed the German couple. Rather than enter the church they had commandeered a long trestle table at the edge of a picnic site and were still indefatigably photographing the building and its architecture.

As we rode back along the Célé, we slowed down to look at the house-frontages of the nearby hamlet of Corn. The War memorial, topped by its heavy grey stone cross, was like any other. But something caught my eye, and I stopped. It was an inscription which not only occupied my mind for the remainder of the cycle-run, but continued to do so, with its unresolved possibilities and implications; and its reminder of our abbey guide. Chiselled out were the words: '. . . *André Bouzou: pris 12 mai, 1944, par les allemands . . . mort Nov. 1945, âge 19: Bergen-Belsen*'.

Zev

Round my neck I generally wear a little half-moon. My wife's, weightier and more striking, is kept for special occasions. Both sides of mine are worn smooth. On hers the signature is still clear: Zev. Part Native American, he lived in Arizona until his home, crammed with carvings and artifacts which made it virtually a museum to his culture, was bulldozed to make way for a freeway. He left America for Rome – swearing never to return.

Exactly a quarter of a century ago I met him in his Aladdin's cave overlooking the Tiber. He had turned two upper apartments into one. The elaborate white marble-work including the mantelpiece, and arched and pillared entrances, he had installed and carved himself. Along the walls hung little Picasso-like oils so rich in pigment they seemed gem-encrusted. Each had, in the bottom corner by way of signature, a half-moon: the tribal emblem of the Blackfoot Indians. He showed us a jewel-box commissioned by Muriel Spark, who lived nearby but was abroad on holiday. Glass cabinets displayed objets d'art, in pride of place a set of exquisitely slender silver-and-shell goblets.

In the centre and spotlit was the scale-model for a palace, complete with guard-house and minarets, for the King of Saudi Arabia. At the last moment they'd realised the surrounding desert was so flat, an extra water-pump would be needed. How hide it, in the middle of nowhere? The solution: a little building with fluted pillars and a dome, circled by date-palms and marked on the plan, *Temple to Poseidon*.

My entrée was Nina Froud, my then literary agent and a dear friend to my wife and myself. Her Marylebone flat was a cosy haven and (she was also a writer of cook books) a famished Scotsman's delight. Through her and in the many languages she spoke, the most stimulating people of disparate cultures and nationalities would be warmly introduced: French to Chinese, playwrights to medical specialists. Staying with us in Edinburgh in Gorbachov's heyday she brought Natasha, who wept as she recited Pushkin in Russian long into the night. Another time Nina took in her stride the appalling sherry which was all we had to offer: 'My dears, just call it a well-travelled Madeira!'

She knew I was to be an observer at the Prix Italia at Bologna, while she would be holidaying in Rome with Ettore Violani, an Italian poet and at that time head of RAI's overseas service, and his wife Franca who had translated my poetry into Italian. They kindly invited me to join them, subsequently: hence my presence, at Zev's.

The other guests included a suntanned Bostonian called Hamilton, cheerfully nicknamed Proscutio, who had flown specially from New York for the occasion: to celebrate the 94th birthday later in the week of Zev's housekeeper Adalgesa. A tiny animated figure in black, she could still take the stairs at a canter. As she rolled the pasta for dinner she bemoaned a lack of sex in her life. Asked when she'd first noticed she chortled: 'Last night'. Adding wistfully, 'Then again, this morning!'

My host and hostess lived in the wooded suburb of Monte Mario. The front door of the apartment was almost obscured by locks and bolts. Ettore revered and collected Renaissance paintings: he was patiently restoring a Bassano landscape. My bedroom was tiny. On the wall opposite my bed, in an oval frame, hung a portrait of the Madonna once ascribed to Leonardo: supposedly the same model as his Virgin of the Rocks. I lay more tense than were any woman of flesh beside me. Whenever I put out the light, I'd hear the whine of a mosquito. Each time I put the light back on, it would settle just out of reach. Until I could see it nowhere on the ceiling or upper wall: it had to be lower down. I got out of bed and gripped my rolled newspaper. Then caught sight of it: perched precisely on the nose of the Madonna.

Nina took me to St Peter's, guiding me clockwise so that Rodin's *The Kiss* (now behind glass), would be unexpected and have its full impact. In the Borghese Gallery I'd my first glimpse of Bernini's *Apollo*, and in the sunny Gardens encountered a new level of composure. Opposite a neat-bummed statue of Aphrodite crouched a Sphinx: to think he hadn't batted an eyelid, down all these centuries. With the symmetry of Michelangelo's marble patterning and the statue of Marcus Aurelius on horseback still on its plinth, the Campidoglio was as beautiful a man-made space as I'd ever seen. Behind shuttered windows: a breath-stoppingly tender sculpture of *Cupid and Psyche*, and *The Dying Gaul*, in the one room. Life from the first butterfly kiss, to the crushed throat.

Afterwards I turned at the far corner of the Square for a last look back – and hesitantly asked a passing tourist, laden with expensive-looking camera equipment, if he'd mind taking one of me with the statue in the background. Peering through my cheap little effort, he took a step back to get everything in – and fell backwards down the steps. 'Are you all right?' I shouted, 'and is my camera okay?' 'Fuck *your* camera!' he yelled. As he picked up his gear, I slunk away.

On the Via Sacra, where Horace encountered his old bore, I kept my nose in the air for fear of doing likewise – and deservedly ended up ankle-deep in horse-shit. Prevented by 'an insufficiency of guardians' from climbing the Palatine Hill, I sat on a slab of white marble, pondering whether Petronius was singularly a product of his age or just had a dirty mind. All this in a Rome shortly to be torn by explosion.

My stay is now remote; peopled by apparitions who might be from a dream – or an unwritten Spark novel. Zev died years ago – Nina herself, this summer. All I have of that particular brief convergence is a flyer for an exhibition: against a black back-ground, his name and 'Ankrum, Oct. 28th 1968'. And those caringly preserved but slowly wearing-away half-moons. Saddened by the circumstances of his uprootedness and his missing out on subsequent shifts of attitude, I visualise Zev emerging from the baths or striding some mythic pantheon, in toga and sandals but lavishly furred and feathered, puffing the pipe of his forebears. Then being transported by time's charioteers, to beam down from among the constellations.

REFLECTIONS

On the Water

Past the stone horses of the Guggenheim
an elderly couple, he tall and wiry,
she dumpy, their thrust seemingly effortless,
pole a green skiff down the Grand Canal.

Like musicians at one with their instruments
theirs is a fusion of concentration and skill,
gravity in their stance, body-weight poised
for each forward motion of the oar.

In their wake the ripples dazzlingly mirror
the palazzi opposite, as though upstream
a school of colourists were skittishly
washing out their brushes and palettes.

Photograph of San Michele

This island of death and cypresses
taken in absolute stillness: see
the pink walls and marble statues,
Renaissance church and monastery;

and beyond, crammed
and crumbling, the mausoleums
with their worn inscriptions
to rich and poor alike,

The image so perfect, impossible
to tell which way up it should be:
which is water, which sky — far less
what may lie under the surface.

Campanile

As
the
early
mist clears
two campaniles
emerge dreamlike
one in now sparkling
air, one underwater
or so it would appear
— its clean-cut lines
quivering amongst
ripples which could
have been drawn by
Guardi or Canaletto
one unlikely feature
of whose paintings
is wholly verifiable:
Venice the only city
where truly the water
retains its cobalt blue
even under a grey sky.

Self Portrait: Man in Red Hat

Here's me looking at you looking at me
looking at you . . . and so ad infinitum.
Or it would be were we both captured
on canvas, hence invulnerable to time.

Ironic how subject to your whim,
in the years ahead (posterity,
as you like to regard it) I'll be the one
(silly hat and all) subject to scrutiny.

How many I wonder will take in
that I'm a mirror image, my features
not yours but their reverse; that archly
raised eyebrow, the wrong one?

Leaving the Accademia

Watching an ageing couple
approach arm in arm, I sense
in their expression a range
of emotions: in conjunction

with pleasure at wonders seen
and a heightened affection
in each other's company,
something of the startled quality

of animals blinking at the light.
Simultaneously you look up,
catch our reflection in the mirror.
Fleetingly, our eyes meet.

Dead Letters

'Next we have Art Pepper who has since died – but who was alive at the time of recording.' On hearing this in a BBC Television feature, it flitted absurdly through my mind that the wording might be in the wake of some contractual tussle (with Gabriel Records, say) and by way of assurance that despite his decease all obligations had been properly met. One way or the other Auntie would have turned up trumps: in those days I still clung to the belief that in such matters, she was a beacon of light in a murky world.

That was before I received a radio contract in a new format whose conditions of engagement contained two convoluted clauses. One granted 'the unlimited right to edit copy alter add to take from adapt or translate the contribution(s) and . . . waive irrevocably any "moral rights" you may have under the laws of any jurisdiction' [sic]. The other assigned to the Corporation 'the complete copyright and all other rights for all purposes (including use in all media now known or which may hereafter become known) everywhere in the contribution(s) for the full period of copyright and any extensions, revivals and renewals thereof'.

The first struck me as rather odd, to put it mildly, for a poem sequence. And with no period specified the latter would presumably allow repeat broadcasts *ad infinitum* (or *ad nauseam*) while waiving the hitherto mandatory repeat fee. Not surprisingly the change had already caused friction. The upshot: if I tore up the contract, another would be issued. I did, and it was. The original wording, though, still seems the norm: gobbledygook apparently in perpetuity.

When the playwright Alexander Reid died in 1982 his wife invited me to choose one of his books as a memento. Although delighted, I was concerned lest I might inadvertantly pick one worth more than was proper. She said I needn't worry: the dealers had already been in to sift out the goodies. I browsed through the remaining shelves and settled on a 1912 impression of *On The Art of the Theatre*, Edward Gordon Craig's epoch-making plea for a return to aesthetic revolution and revelation. Its contents included letters on the Theatre in Russia, Germany and England followed by extended dialogues between a Playgoer and the Stage-Director on the Theatre at large and Stage Design in particular, and ended with an essay on 'The Exquisite and the Precious'. There were black-and-white illustrations of Craig's costumes and settings for Shakespeare, the *Electra* and a *Masque of London*.

In the margins, in neatly-slanting pencil, were French equivalents to English terms in the text. And at the front of the book there was a squiggle in red ink through the dedication to William Blake – and written in:

> *(Note for translator)*
> *For the French Edition I*
> *intend to write a new*
> *dedication –*
> > *EGC*

On the fly-leaf in the same handwriting but in black pen:

> *To the translator.*
>
> *Dear Sir or Madam – Your task is not easy;*
> *but I hope something in this book of mine*
> *will appeal sufficiently to you to arouse*
> > *in you an interest in the work.*
> > *Then all will be well –*
> *I shall be ever ready to be of assistance*

to you should there be anything in
the book which seems vague to you

You will notice that I have used several
words which are not what is considered to
belong to 'the best English'.
Do not mind that – do not be
afraid of them.
There are slang expressions here and there –
do not make them sound prettier –

Our aim is to express not
to make pretty sentences –

I wish you every success in your
work – & I hope some pleasure.

> *Yours sincerely*
> *Gordon Craig,*
> *January 1913, Florence*

Surprised no interest had been shown in it, I accepted the book with some excitement. Its whole argument reveals this urge to express, not 'make pretty sentences', as a bulwark of Craig's rigorous yet lavishly futuristic as against realistic approach to theatrical design and presentation. The cloth-bound volume is by me as I write, alongside two old favourites, Walter Baynham's *The Glasgow Stage* (1892) and a battered copy of *Stage Reminiscences of An Old Stager* (1866), and a pedantic work on *Dramatic Technique* by a Professor at Yale University: its stilted sample scenarios, all but unreadable, making what I coughed up for it all the more galling.

I've since seen so many editions of Craig's work advertised that I've come to accept that rather than a rarity, he is constantly being offloaded. (A parallel, Shaw's *St Joan*: in my youthful browsing I thought I had struck gold, until I deduced that the original imprint must have been large enough to supply every second-hand bookshop in the land several times over.) My copy of *On the Art of the Theatre* was in any case not <u>Fine in dw</u> but had a torn spine and no dust-cover. And for all I knew, the annotations – so pleasing to me – might to the trade be seen as a blemish. That suited me. Rather than worry about its monetary value I enjoyed having at my fingertips these injunctions, in his own hand. No other name is on the volume; nor is there any way of knowing who owned it in between.

After Genevieve Reid's death I received unsolicited through the post a Modern Scottish Literature catalogue. It indexed first editions ranging from Butlin and Byrne to Tranter and Trocchi, by way of Dunn and Dunnett: a ubiquitous poke of chips. I especially liked a description of an Epilogue for the American Edition of Alasdair Gray's *Something Leather* in the author's hand which ended: 'Two sheets fine; the third creased, as in retrieved from the bin creased!' Then something caught my eye:

> CONN, Stewart. *Thunder in the Air.* Akros 1967. Poetry. Inscribed by the author to the poet and playwright Alexander Reid and his wife Genevieve. Laid in is a 400 word tls from the author to Reid in which he thanks the same for allowing him to read his Bruno novel (the novel was never published) . . . Conn also sympathises in the letter with the six novelists waiting for the Arts Council to decide on a book award: 'It must be murder now for the poor novelists . . .'

Here I named a writer I seemingly saw as not 'in the running', then went on: 'Mackay Brown strikes me as the one who has, within the wording of the thing, most "contributed towards" anything – a valid and excitingly new prose style for short stories.' So there! <u>Book: Wrappers. Near Fine. Letter: Fine. For both: £20.</u> I'm pretty sure that if the choice were to be made over again, I'd go as I did then for *A Calendar of Love.* And had the other writer named read my comments or glimpsed this catalogue, rather than take umbrage or turn homicidal, he'd have regarded it as little skin off his nose – especially as he has shown every sign since (mainly through a nom-de-plume) of laughing all the way to the bank. Yet neither of us should have been put in a position of potential embarrassment, however minimal, by the public airing of a view expressed confidentially, in a private letter. What if something more forceful or hurtful, libelous even, had been said? What indeed might the remainder of the letter contain? If it and the pamphlet were sold then in whose hands, tactful or otherwise, are they now?

My friendly neighbourhood second-hand bookseller suggested that my signature on the book wasn't necessarily damaging, but it would have been better if I'd 'been someone'. And that its being in green ink was scarcely aesthetically enhancing. He moved on to say that if the purchaser of a bureau finds in it a bond for $1m, this isn't rightfully his unless he bought both bureau and contents. Letters or cuttings are however so commonly lodged in books or used as bookmarks, that while in theory buying the one needn't guarantee your right to the other, in common practice their going together is tacitly accepted. He saw no quibble in other words, about the passing on or further offer for sale of the letter.

But he drew a clear distinction between what a letter or document is physically written on and its content: the words themselves. As these remain the writer's property, clearance must be sought prior to publication: whether for letters held privately, or (as part of a bequest say) in a Library. A reader or researcher may be given access. But before quoting from them, even in an authorised biography, permission must be granted by the letter-writer – or his or her estate. In other words, from whoever holds the copyright.

The holders of copyright where this volume was concerned could not have been more spontaneously and generously supportive. Others can by contrast be greedy or dogs-in-the-manger, demanding that what is written represents the truth precisely as they see it or wish it seen. A lot may hinge on the perceived integrity or bias of a biographer. The golden rule of course is never (at any rate – back to Art Pepper – not while still alive) sign away what could become a free gift. Against that it can be costly to assume that copyright (or ownership) is invested in you: for instance if it's for the lyrics of a Paul McCartney song.

With regard to that catalogue – or my reproducing part of it here – I suspect the wordage is so tiny in any case that it isn't worth making a song and dance about. Certainly no point in being litigious or going busting noses. In the present context I like to think it can be regarded as an amicable *quid pro quo*. But worth bearing in mind that what A writes privately to B about C's novel (or love-life) may end up being read by biographer D and nosey-parkers E to Z alike. So *en garde*, unless you get your kicks by spilling the beans posthumously – one way I suppose, of writing for posterity. Although so much in print these days is so scabrous, any eventual frisson may be diminished.

Gordon Craig died in 1966, aged 94. Needless to say I was no more at liberty in this essay to quote the margin-note to his French translator than had it been in the form of a letter found inside the book. I'm delighted to say permission was instantly and courteously – and freely – granted by his grand-daughter Ellen Craig. As for the volume itself, its damaged binding could be restored to pristine condition should I so wish. All in all, I hope Craig's appearance in this context doesn't seem to breach the spirit of things. I'd hate to think of his ghost (if not his estate) venting upon me the fiery-dragon fervency he was known for when he was alive and Ellen Terry's blood coursed in his veins.

Clearance of the spoken or broadcast word can lead to further complexities over copyright and broadcast performance. Having had to make phone-calls costing quite a proportion of the difference between the sum on offer (increasingly, these days, in retrospect) and what the guidelines decree, mine is very much a divided self: to fight tooth and nail, or to throw in the towel. The music world is even more labyrinthine: sanity there is I suspect best served by closing one's eyes and hoping for the best possible outcome, in the worst of all possible worlds. And of course by having a good agent – or I suppose, a couple of strong minders.

I enjoy the account of Yonty Solomon being booked to play a Beethoven piano concerto at a Butlin's anniversary concert. The top-brass were in the front row. During the lengthy orchestral introduction the soloist sat impassive, hands on his lap. Sir Billy grew more and more agitated; then leaned across to hiss at his business manager: 'Is there some trouble over Mr Solomon's fee?' At that moment the distinguished guest's fingers resoundingly hit the key-board. Everyone could sit back, and relax.

A Writer's Lot

You're a writer? Spell somethin'!
– SAM GOLDWYN –

[1]

I am at home. In my small study. I've just begun a year's unpaid leave of absence from my day-job, in order to write. And am still trying on my new identity. We have painters in. Big Eck hovers. 'Mr Conn, mind if I ask you a personal question?' 'Fire away.' 'What do you do?' 'How do you mean?' 'Your job, like. My mate says you're with the BBC along the road there. I says I wisnae sure.'

I nod. As I do so I remember my new identity. 'What *do* you do, but? You an actor?' 'No, not an actor.' 'A producer then. Or a director . . . furra Tellie.' I shake my head. He grimaces. 'What else *is* there? You're no a lighting-man? Or wanna they grips or something?'

'I'm the one everyone forgets.' 'Eh?' 'Behind the scenes.' He looks blank. 'The writer. I'm a *writer*.' 'What do you write, but?' 'Poems mainly, plus plays.' He looks glum. 'For Radio now and then . . . Occasionally the Tellie.' Honour is satisfied.

Next morning first thing, Big Eck appears. 'Eh Mr Conn, mind what you was telling us yesterday? Awright if I ask you something?' 'Go ahead.' 'Well I go hame and have a shufty at the *TV Guide*. Top to tail. *Radio Times* ditto – it's the daughter-in-law brings it in. Nae sign. So I thought, I must ask Mr Conn. The big question.' He looks me in the eye. 'Like tae tell us, whit name is it you write under?'

[2]

Dundee. The train pulls into the station. I'm met by two girl students, who ask would I like a bite to eat before the reading. I say that'd be great. We find a café, chat over a bowl of soup and a sandwich. They explain that as the Literary Society is still relatively new they can't guarantee a big turn-out, but that there should be at least a keen nucleus there.

We leave the café, head for their car. We get in, them in front, and set off. I'm sitting there in a dwam, going over my opening words. Then become conscious that the girl in the passenger seat has squirmed round and is looking at me quizzically. She seems to come to a conclusion, and half-frowns. Then speaks.

'To me you don't look like a poet. You look more like a lorry-driver.'

[3]

I've just joined the train. Yesterday I was in and around Aberdeen. I'd booked a seat from there. But there came the offer of a lift to Stonehaven, where I stayed in a B & B. After breakfast, a bracing walk along the cliffs to Dunnottar Castle and back. The clear air of the Mearns. The capacious skies of a James Morrison painting. The overlay of a rainbow, out to sea . . . As we picked up speed I got my book out. The man opposite was immersed in his overcoat. He spoke:
Jammy.
Sorry?
You, mate. That seat's reserved.
I know. I reserved it.
No way. You've just got on. It's reserved from Fishy City.
Simpler to leave it at that than try to explain. I opened my book.

Going to Edinburgh?

I nodded.

I've a London connection. Hope I make it. Another there for Hull.

Hull?

Hull's home.

How . . . via London?

Car's there. Got a call saying they wanted me to do some test driving for them. At short notice. In Oil-ville-that-was. Had to sign the contract, get the sleeper from London.

As I turned back to my book he added:

You on pleasure, or business?

Business, actually . . .

What doing?

Before I could bite it back:

Some workshops. Writers' workshops.

You're a writer?

That's right.

He pondered this then peered at me:

Will I have heard of you?

That's most unlikely.

I mean . . . are you a famous writer?

I shook my head. He looked momentarily crestfallen, then perked up.

Not even an infamous writer?

I'm afraid not. Sorry.

No sweat.

He pushed his hands into the sleeves of his overcoat and closed his eyes. In next to no time, as the train hurtled along the coastline, he was snoring.

[4]

River Falls, Wisconsin. First port of call on a reading and lecture tour of the Mid-West. Purpose and nature of stay: to be a Visiting Poetry Professor. A Real Writer. Although here everybody seems to be a Professor. Most of them seemingly married, now or at some time in the past, to each other. Yesterday I had three classes, and gave a reading. Afterwards a walk along the crystal-clear Kinnickinnic with Thomas R. Smith, a fine lyricist who shares the French poet Francis Ponge's belief that artists 'have to open a workshop and take the world in for repairs'.

So far no need (as I was warned there might be) for a placard round my neck saying, *'Visiting Poet: please talk to me'*. Further sessions planned for this morning. At breakfast my host points out a crimson-feathered cardinal on a bough outside. A chipmunk crosses the road opposite. As the bells of academe sound, I do my final preparation.

I am excited at what may await me: the first class consists I've been told of 'fourteen female sophomores, all poetry lovers'. May they be attractively brilliant . . . brilliantly attractive. This is the life. I add an extra skoosh of *Tuscany Per Uomo*. I grab my bag. I am walking on air.

As I leave the house I hear my host bemoan: 'What a waste. All those succulent young creatures . . . and one old man.'

Darkness into Light

Years ago I was approached by a writer friend compiling a book on happiness. It was to contain descriptions of times or instances of outstanding happiness in different people's lives. And he wanted me to contribute. For someone not in a state of extended bliss the solution would presumably be to delve into the past. But things can be filtered or rarified by the passage of time. How readily could the experience be recaptured – even if there had been one? Jane Austen's *Emma* wasn't too encouraging: 'Perfect happiness, even in memory, is not common.' It was as if my head had been shoved into a byke of bees. If I were to come up with something, how do it justice? And what would it have to register on the Richter scale to qualify?

As it turned out my choice proved remarkably (or unremarkably) easy. I chose a holiday with my wife in Haute Provence, not long after we were married. A remote world of fragrances, of blue skies and white peaks; of lavender-clumps like hassocks for Provençal ladies. As luck had it too, my task was already done – in the form of a poem sequence with its focal point a Chinese tower high on a hill overlooking a chapel. From it could be seen the swerve of the valley, the mountains pink beyond, then the blueness of the sky. Goat-bells could be heard chinking in the breeze. The village clock struck every hour twice. Time held in abeyance; harmony

135

(and oneness) attained, the impenetrable blueness the more precious for its transience.

But what of my friend's anthology? So far as I know it never bore fruit. Maybe it proved too great a chore. Certainly before finishing it, he was locked in a deep depression. Paradoxical, given that his raw material was happiness. Although maybe all too explicable: was he trying to alleviate, or escape, its grip? Or was the infusion of the delights of others simply too much to bear? A further irony was that the would-be compiler was the playwright Alexander Reid, my conversations with whom were constantly enlivened by his memories of Neil Gunn and his 'atoms of delight'. Alec's philosophising could be so convoluted as to make pursuit tricky. When he gravitated to Gunn it was like trying to follow one of many deer-tracks through a pine-forest, with cones whacking you in the face at each turning off.

The more I'd familiarised myself with Gunn's novels and *The Atom of Delight*, and joined in its autobiographical pursuit of moments of 'cleansing' insight, the more illusory – or elusory – they became. I felt increasingly like a child putting out one hand, then cupping the other over it, to catch a moonbeam. I warm to Gunn's entry into the mind of the growing boy, not least in his recurring tussle with the salmon in the pool. There is also his ability to build a picture of our ancestry, of our tribal forebears and the wisdom handed down for us to preserve and pass on. Informing this are his compassion and understanding, and a belief that there is a meaning behind it all. And what ultimately validates his 'moments' is their grounding in real experience to which one can relate, yet which 'remains like a radioactive atom at delight's centre'.

On holiday once with his wife Daisy, Gunn found a well, its crystal water made invisible by fern-fronds intercepting the light. From this reminder of Gaelic legend stemmed the quest of Peter, a middle-aged Professor of Ancient History, which comprises *The Well at the World's End*. Besides depicting the renewal of a marriage the novel, in common with so much of Gunn's fiction, is both spiritual autobiography and a study of levels of consciousness.

At one point Alick, one of three whisky-smugglers Peter falls in with, tells of being rescued from drowning by a friend – in circumstances reminiscent of a real-life experience Gunn once had in France. Alick describes the feeling that subsequently came over him: he knew ' . . . that there exists an order of things outside our conception of time . . . There was nothing at all in the ordinary sense "religious" about this experience; but what is astonishing, I think, is that there was nothing personal . . . as I sat down . . . I was overcome by a divine, a delicious sense of humour'.

Alan Spence, in an article on Gunn, sees this as describing with a beautiful simplicity and directness what Gunn means by his 'timeless moments': that 'sudden awakening to reality, an intuition and a certainty, direct *seeing*, the doors of perception cleansed'. Again, it is Gunn's own character which gives to elements that might otherwise have remained remote their mellowness; his buoyancy which invests them with human form; with the inner strength and serenity, as Spence saw it, which had so profound an impact on the younger writer.

Gunn seems to me to exemplify André Breton's claim that 'all great prose partakes of the nature of poesie': not just stylistically but in the sense of bringing light. *Light* meaning *enlightenment*. The more I read of today's prose, much of it self-servingly crude, gratuitously violent and morally vacuous, the sadder it seems that the qualities in Gunn which are most vital and which our society most desperately needs should be among those which make him unfashionable. It is not that I'd proscribe violence or discord, or disapprove any depiction of the brute side of man's nature; but that rather than a wallowing in them, I would advocate some transforming principle: a moral insight and vision to counter (as ultimately in Dostoyevsky) the degradation of the pit.

Gunn remains for me one of the Old Men of the Tribe, a communal repository for Wisdom. I recall meeting him and his brother John in Edinburgh, and under my own steam visiting him in North Kessock. I clearly recall Neil, head tilted, an amber glint from the glass in his hand, the slight burr of his speech, the dry laugh with volumes behind it. As darkness drew in the fire glowed, and the light was switched on – thanks to the power from the metal pylons I naively said must spoil their view, but which his wife Daisy said were among the most beautiful things she could think of. It is now as though those moments with him existed in some kind of Plato's cave, shadows cast on the wall and the sense of a veil being drawn, the reality as against the image momentarily visible; before the instant had gone, and everything became unreal again.

On a last visit with my own wife – long after Daisy's death and shortly before Neil's – he was at a sadly low ebb, complaining that memory was playing him tricks. I sensed a deep hurt in him, that his work had gone out of fashion: if his books were in print at all, they were critically discountenanced. Allied to the *inter*nationalism of his nationalism, this may have been one reason why the founding of the SAC International

Fellowship in his honour meant so much to him: these two words meaning more to him, he told me, than any other.

Once with the angst of youth I told him I had finished writing something, and was worried because nothing else had begun gnawing at me. He gave a knowing nod: 'That's the best time there is: enjoy it while you can.' In due course he became something of a guru (almost a father) figure. Our first son, born ten days before Neil's death in January '73, was called Arthur – in part after Young Art: something Neil knew we had in mind. I'd have liked them to meet . . . Young Art and Old Hector. As for me, there's still no one I more wish I could have been taken fishing by than Neil Gunn – with salmon-rod, or bent pin.

I derive much pleasure from the fiction of my Scottish contemporaries, from James Kelman's darkly luminous masterpieces to the pick of Alasdair Gray's exotic cornucopia. Douglas Dunn's 'secret communities' seethe with torn loyalties, immured in conspiratorial seclusion and realised with a poet's perception. The finesse of Bernard MacLaverty's insights is arrestingly welded to 'your man's' lovely way with words and an ability to entertain, yoked to a moral sense which arouses compassion for the characters in their psychological confinement. These writers enhance our understanding of ourselves as well as the world around us.

Recent years have seen the emergence of a number of dazzlingly different writers, from Frank Kuppner to A.L. Kennedy. Kuppner can generate remarkable feeling in the face of a seemingly sceptical detachment from his subject-matter and, within his intricate constructs, a web of I suspect not always instantly detectable humour. Besides endowing her characters with scintillating lucidity of language and mind-set, Kennedy for me not only illumines those peopling her fictional worlds, but consistently challenges and changes my perceptions.

It can be difficult, when what is new and compelling is also shocking and contradictory, to detect continuity in consecutive generations of writers. More often than not they see their predecessors as having hurled down a gauntlet rather than passed on a baton, or representing an ideology to be overturned. Many a writer of whatever age feels impelled to break allegiance to a tradition which seems inhibiting or restrictive – or simply jaded. Others (again across a broad spectrum) have shown a rewarding readiness to confront the past and its monoliths head on, and add an individual imprint: from the astute forays of the prolific Allan Massie to James Robertson's marvellously impassioned and thought-provoking first novel *The Fanatic*.

When Alan Spence urges the importance of continuity, what he advocates is neither naive nor linguistically retrograde but 'the continued striving for the light'. Not surprisingly, in that for years now Spence has been practising meditation under the guidance of the Indian master Sri Chinmoy, for *light* again read *enlightenment*. But no more for Spence than when it was said dismissively of Gunn does this imply impracticality or any retreat into 'a personal mysticism'. Meditation sharpens rather than etherealises his vision. I'm confident Spence adheres equally to Dostoyevsky's dictum, 'compassion is the chief law of human existence': the more crucially when lives are threatened or encompassed by the forces of darkness.

With an ear sensitive to everyday speech-rhythms, much of his work (something he shares with the more high-octane and male-oriented William McIlvanney) penetrates the pain and potential for hurt of a boy growing up not in Gunn's highland strath but in a harsh urban setting. Of his stories graphing age, one enters the mind of an old man in the overheated globe of Glasgow's Kibble Palace: all life, a transition. Although those in his most recent volume, *Stone Garden*, venture further afield, its pivotal figures remain temporary exiles or escapees from Glasgow, linked to that city as inextricably as Spence seems to be, by a potent umbilical tie.

He reveals a constant desire to be reconciled with the past. But this is seen in the perspective of the present, and what lies ahead. Nor does he falsify or glamorise his moments of epiphany. He may exquisitely recall a candle in whose soft glow 'the things on the table stood illumined like objects in some strange painting'. But later in the same story the boy is brought back to earth, having omitted to rest the candle-stub on anything: 'In burning right down it had scorched the table-top. It had made a round hole, the formica cracked and buckled round about it, like a volcanic crater.'

That there should be something incorruptible about Spence's fictional world is no surprise. His ultimate concern (in common with those others I've mentioned) is with the moral grace-notes and continuity of other folks' (and our) lives. As a storyteller he never severs his link with real emotions and experience or the human heartbeat, no matter how ominous, even alienating that may be.

In 'Nessun Dorma' a student is asked what he thinks is the finest music in the world. His answer echoes Fionn's: 'The music of what happens.' This sums up, not only in a social or aesthetic context but within an intuitive and spiritual dimension, Spence's rare gift. And what it all boils down to in the end: *'The music of what happens. Stay tuned.'*

The Dominion of Fancy

Even in a profession generously endowed with flamboyancy and eccentricity, John Henry Alexander stands out. Born in Dunbar in 1796, the second of five brothers, he was schooled mainly in Edinburgh. When his watch-maker father retired to Glasgow he was apprenticed to an uncle, a hosier and glover at the foot of the Candleriggs. In his spare time the young Alexander read the memoirs of Garrick, Macklin and as he put it 'other eminent members of the histrionic art'. Infatuated with the theatre he took up acting and distinguished himself 'by giving out the performances at the end of the play, and addressing the audiences in case of emergency'. Turning professional he trod the boards in Aberdeen, Ayr, Carlisle and Scarborough, besides spending some ten years in Edinburgh where in 1817 he married, before reappearing on the Glasgow stage as Rashleigh Osbaldistone in a touring production of *Rob Roy*.

Since the early years of the century Glasgow's main theatre, in Dunlop Street, had been in decline. The city was changing: what had been drab lanes and patches of waste ground when it was built were now ornamented with pleasure gardens. Nearby Queen Street had handsome new villas where wealthy merchants lived. They wanted to patronise a theatre that was more fashionable and more profitable to its shareholders. A site was found in Queen Street itself. Subscription shares were sold and the elegantly proportioned Theatre Royal, with its ionic columns and pilasters, its interior vestibules and boxes, was completed.

As the new theatre became established Dunlop Street deteriorated until by 1821 it was little better than a circus, ranging from a New-Year Harlequinade to Melodramas and Horsemanship. That year Alexander had become manager of the theatre in Carlisle which he would retain for twelve years, coupling it with Dumfries. In 1822, keen to make his mark in Glasgow, he added the Dunlop Street building, by now sadly run down. Almost immediately, fresh competition appeared on his doorstep. A Mr Kinloch took another theatre in Dunlop Street, the Caledonian, where he put on an admirably mounted piece based on Pierce Egan's *Tom and Jerry.* This made a profit of over £2000, from which Kinloch went from strength to strength.

In 1825 Alexander heard the Caledonian was on the market. Eager to add it to his circuit, he proposed terms. Getting wind of this Francis Seymour, the stage manager and leading actor at the Theatre Royal, urged his manager Mr Byrne to lodge a counter-bid. When Byrne showed no interest Seymour decided to go it alone. He had a close friend, a Bailie Lang, who had some interest in the Caledonian. In Lang's ironmongery shop in the Trongate, agreement was reached: a portion of the annual rent was paid in advance, and the keys were handed over. Seymour instructed that repairs begin immediately. Forty-eight hours later Alexander, having hastened from Dumfries by *poste-chaise,* arrived on the scene and found to his chagrin that Seymour had stolen a march on him.

But as Alexander was leaving he noticed a cart being loaded with bales from some sort of storehouse beneath the main building. Exploring where this led to he found an unexpectedly spacious cellar, occupied by a cotton-dealer and a potato-salesman. Confident this would convert into a place of amusement he made such a good offer for the lease that the pair were prepared not just to give up their tenancy, but to vacate the premises on the spot.

Who could open to the public first? Seymour engaged a company of actors, mostly from the Royal. At the end of a frenetic month the theatre was transformed. Where above the pit there had been only a gallery at the far end of the house, the Caledonian now boasted side boxes from the gallery to the stage. The pit itself was re-seated, the seats covered with red cloth. Most strikingly the arch of gas-jets over the proscenium which had blackened the finely decorated ceiling was replaced by twenty-four cut-glass lustres round the sweep of the boxes.

Meanwhile Alexander's crew from Carlisle worked wonders. The below-ground stage area was small but neat, the big drawback its low ceiling which meant the seats also had to be very low. These all ran horizontally, as in a fair-ground booth, and were portioned off into boxes, pit and gallery by ropes drawn tightly across. In due course the less scrupulous members of the audience would cut the ropes and push forward; so that eventually they were replaced by heavy chains 'upon which the knife of any knavish butcher or shoemaker would have less effect'.

Alexander put out a very good bill, lamenting that the Caledonian had slipped through his fingers but claiming he had fitted up 'as good a temple of the drama' as the one upstairs. Aware that under the patent laws he could not style the establishment a theatre he informed the public that with their permission he would call it the Dominion of Fancy – as he intended and hoped to succeed 'in tickling both their ears and their fancy during the season'.

Seymour opened with *Macbeth* and Alexander, a few days later, with *The Battle of the Inch.* The upstairs production was marred by the shouts of soldiery, the clashing of swords, the clanging of dish covers and the braying of drums down below. As the actor playing Macbeth was bracing himself for the dagger speech the Highlanders only a few feet beneath him went at it hammer and tongs. As if this was not enough the smoke and fumes of the 'blue fire' used for the fight scenes started to drift chokingly up through the chinks in the planks.

On a subsequent run, as the curtain rose in the Dominion of Fancy, a brass band engaged by Seymour started off and played throughout the evening, completely drowning the words of the actors below. The tunes were the jauntiest in their repertoire, with the trombones instructed not to play *piano* or take too many bars rest. For a while and far from harming either box-office, the anticipation of such spontaneous effects drew crammed and delighted audiences.

Soon though respectable playgoers, tiring of such antics, started to patronise the Theatre Royal in Queen Street. At this stage both managers petitioned the Glasgow magistrates to devise some regulation whereby each could protect his livelihood. It was decreed that Seymour should play four nights a week and Alexander only two – but these Saturday and Monday, the best of the week. Both appealed to the Court of Session, who merely ratified the decision.

During one production in the 'cellar', as he disdainfully called it, Seymour's stage crew prised up the planks and poured water down through them, forcing members of Alexander's audience to put up umbrellas to protect themselves. By way of retaliation chanting crowds would group at the stage door of the Caledonian. There were further appeals to the magistrates, who said that if they had any more complaints they would simply have both places closed down.

Knowing *Der Freischutz* had just had a successful run in Edinburgh, Seymour bought all the costumes and props and announced he would open with it the following Tuesday. But Alexander had played the piece in Carlisle not long before. By Saturday the walls of the city were placarded with bills for it that evening – in the Dominion of Fancy. In addition, 'treasury' day was Seymour's favourite day to be 'indisposed'. There was no sign of the 'ghost walking'. Only after a call-boy was sent to his house with a strike threat were the wages paid. Seymour, incensed, demanded everything possible be done to disrupt Alexander.

Placed at various parts of the stage where the flooring could be easily lifted, Seymour's minions caught hold of the Dragon by the tail until it was burnt out, then let it fly across the stage in smoke and darkness. They upset the chase of the skeleton huntsmen; and tangled the lines holding the backdrop for the enchantment scene – releasing them with a run that nearly extinguished the footlights. The final curtain came down with such a crash, the dust was suffocating. An enraged Alexander stepped forward and appealed 'as to how long he and his brother huntsmen were to be interrupted in the sport by the misdeeds of *foreign* intruders' – Seymour being Irish. So things continued. But neither could complain about his receipts for the season. At one point *Tom and Jerry* played both houses simultaneously for a month – so successfully that Queen Street was deserted and its manager, Mr Byrne, left. Seymour applied successfully for the theatre.

His first discovery was that Byrne had skedaddled owing six months' rent, and with the keys to the theatre in his pocket. Seymour had to make his first entrance through a window in the green room, at the back of the building. Real catastrophe was to follow. Early in 1829 a light, misty vapour was seen rising from the roof of the Theatre Royal. By the time the fire-engines arrived, the interior was a mass of flames. Not a particle of the building, or a piece of Seymour's property, was saved. The proprietors' losses were covered partly by insurance, but Seymour's were nearly £2000. From a fancy ball held for his benefit he realised close on £1000. At midnight there was a whisper that the manager had disappeared, the money with him. He had made no attempt to pay his considerable debts or even for the hire of the hall. He was arrested that night on board the steamer about to sail for Belfast. Paying off the alert creditor who had tracked him, he got off scot-free without having to satisfy the others.

Returning in October with influential backing, Seymour opened a theatre in York Street – only to close ignominiously eighteen months later. Alexander who had meanwhile taken over the Caledonian (literally a step up in the world) now succeeded in transferring the patent of the Theatre Royal to himself. Still Seymour continued with a series of prosecutions against him. On the most petty fancied infringement of his rights, he would have Alexander and his company up before the Justices – often more than twice a week, with the outcome usually the standard penalty of £50 each. On the whole Alexander suffered no harm from this persecution. The fines were never enforced, and he had public sympathy on his side.

In physique and temperament the two rivals could scarcely have been less alike. The first volume of the 'Opera Glass', dedicated to Alexander, gave this graphic portrait:

> JOHN HENRY ALEXANDER is in the midst of his Company like Saul among the sons of Israel. He is a tall man, a stout man, and a rich man, or John Henry speaketh untruly – tall, stout and strong, meaneth *great*, then he is a *great* man, ergo, Alexander the Great, or the Great Alexander! *Maximum Alexander secundus.* Hear, O earth, and tremble! – John Henry Alexander is a Scotchman according to the English definition of the phrase – He is a bonny Scot – a cautious Scot – a money-making Scot – and a *booing* Scot (now John Henry has a very particular *bow*, like a pedlar hitching his pack upon his shoulders – the chin saying suddenly to the breast, How-dye-do?). His complexion is of the dingy shade, between the sallow and the cadaverous and his chin perching upward, like an ante-triangle, toward his peaked proboscis, his lips are thin, wide and compressed, his lungs stentorian. John Henry is an absolute man, a mighty man in his own esteem, a vain man, and a timid man – and it seemeth as though he said in his heart, There is none like me unto all the Earth. He never looks at the boxes save over the prompter's shoulder, seldom deigns to glance at the pit, and his words are thrown to the feet of his dearly beloved gods – nevertheless, he knoweth every face, every night, that is within the walls of his Theatre; he will tell

you the colour of your coat, the expression of your eye, and whether its intent be wicked or charitable. John Henry neither liveth in the world nor of the world, he liveth in himself, and in his own property, enveloped in the mightiness of his Palace. He is lord of all he surveys. He is an autocrat over a dozen slaves, and his merits as a player, are they not written in the preceding pages of the O.G.!
– Farewell, John Henry Alexander.

The preceding notice advised, 'Ye hae had a gie deal o' experience now, but still ye are a young man, an' may greatly improve'. As for his rival:

FRANCIS SEYMOUR is a little round sharp-eyed porky man. He has neither caution, foresight, nor memory; but he has a heart, and that heart is 'in the right place,' but his pocket is placed on the wrong side, and (curse the elements!) that pocket is an empty one. Little Frank is all bustle and promise, and, in the overflowing goodness of his heart, he forgets more than he promises. But when he is *in hand*, his hand performs faster than his mouth can promise. Frank Seymour is a prodigal in his generosity, and it has injured his character for justice. He is a man at heart, but a child in business . . . His intentions are honest, but his abilities are bankrupt . . . Frank, let thy promise be behind thy purse. Frank constitutionally has a little of the *blarney*, a spice of his country. He is a rush-forward unthinking daredevil – The worst word he has to say to his company is *gentlemen*, and those gentlemen are all *his managers*. Farewell, Frank, thou art a good actor, and a good little fellow. Sing the old stave,

Hence opposition : rascals 'tis in vain;
For, though I'm down, I'll soon be up again.

1832 was disastrous. Asiatic cholera came here for the first time. Alexander engaged Kean. But his stock company was stigmatised as 'execrable, the very worst, perhaps, that have ever played the legitimate drama in this city, and heaven knows we have been frequently but poorly off in this respect'. On the first night there were no more than five people in the boxes, six in the pit, thirteen in the gallery. Things kept going downhill. Eventually it reached the point when, announcing a new play, Alexander was pelted with vegetables. His method was

> to direct everybody, players, scene shifters, and gas-men, saying, for instance, audibly, 'Come down here, sir.' 'Stand you there, sir.' 'McStuart, that's not your place.' 'Hold your head up, sir.' 'Speak out.' Never for a moment did he allow the audience to forget that he was manager. He beat time to the orchestra; he spoke to the musicians; he sang the music for other people, and he spoke their words. In theatrical parlance, his greatest delight was 'to show the company up'.

In February 1845 he took his benefit. There was a bumper house, and the performances were received 'with the most flattering marks of approbation'. At the end, there was a universal call for Alexander. Eventually he stepped forward:

> 'I had no intention of addressing you this evening, but the general call which has been made has altered my intentions . . . As Caleb Balderstone says – excuse me saying a few words in Scotch; it is our native language – "Mony a sair day I hae had t'keep up the credit o' the house; I have laboured late and early, for suffrance is the badge of all our tribe". I have been called a tyrant by my enemies – for every man has his enemies, and I have mine – but I have also the philosophy to despise them – because I have laboured for you, and have been strict in seeing that all did their duty . . . I love my art; but I feel my lungs are getting weak, and that I am unable to encounter its fatigues. I have gone through the most arduous season I have ever known in my life. It has continued seven months, during which I have spent daily thirteen hours in the theatre, and been only once out of Dunlop Street *[great cheering]*.
>
> 'I am disgusted, sunk, and grieved. I expended an immense amount of money in building this theatre; I erected it for your accommodation, and after my own taste, at a time when I had no opposition, and in the hope that I would reap the advantage; but Glasgow cannot support more than one theatre *[laughter and cries of, "It can support three or four"]*. I

say it again, Glasgow cannot support more than one theatre. I am going to deprive you of this theatre: I think it possible I may never appear here again. During the last season, I have played one hundred and twenty nights without a star, and, like a skilful pilot, brought my vessel safely into port, and am now retiring in the zenith of my power.

'I have only one regret: I cannot leave the theatre behind; I must have a rent, a heavy rent for my property, to remunerate me for my outlay; and, if a few bad farmers were to get in, they might spoil my crops *[great laughter]*. I am thinking of making an arcade from Stockwell Street through the theatre *[loud shouts of laughter]*, if I can get the neighbouring proprietors to agree; but nothing is positively fixed on. I thank you all most kindly, and beg leave most respectfully to bid you farewell.'

He left the stage to cheering which the *Dramatic Review* took with a pinch of salt: 'We cannot believe it. It is contrary to nature, that a man of such unflagging industry and unflinching vanity should permit the candle of his fame to be snuffed out thus.' So it proved. But the years ahead were hard: no stars and by all accounts a poor company. By this time too, his voice had become cracked and discordant. Lowering his prices had no impact: the middle and lower orders had better entertainment, at even lower prices, elsewhere. Then came a supreme error. When an actor he had intended for the role proved 'too cumbersome', he took over Romeo.

Alexander's appearance as the love-sick swain was the signal for a storm of ironical cheers. Shout upon shout of derisive laughter greeted him throughout the earlier scenes, and the climax was reached when in the third act the Friar summoned him to appear, crying, 'Come forth, thou *fearful* man'. When Mr Alexander had fallen to the ground, 'taking the measure of an unmade grave,' the uproar became so great that quite unmindful of his being supposed to be lying unconscious, Mr Alexander suddenly raised his head from the stage, and thus addressed his adversaries: 'I know, I know,' said he, 'You think I can't play Romeo – I know I'm not so young as I was – *[ironical shouts of "Hear, hear"]* – but I have played it all over the world – *[a cry of "Anywhere else, Aleck!"]* – and with the best actresses, and thank God, I can play it still when there is a necessity. 'I have been called an egoist. I am an egoist, but I know my profession and can play on it, like Paganini on the one string of his violin, and to that you are indebted to the proper management of the theatre. Now!' Then throwing himself once more on the ground he resumed his dialogue with the Nurse – 'Speakest thou of Juliet? how is't with her?' Here the shouts in the gallery were resumed. Alexander got up once more and turned on his foes – 'If you treat me civilly I shall do the same to you in return, but when roused you will find I am a lion.' He paused, and glared defiance. Then he lay down again on the stage, and as Romeo, inquired of the Nurse, 'Where is she?' During the entire evening the fight was constantly being renewed.

On Saturday 17th February 1849 the Theatre Royal in Dunlop Street was filled to overflowing. Admission to the upper gallery had been reduced to threepence, and it was crowded with youngsters who had saved their pennies to see *The Surrender of Calais*. At some time between seven and eight o'clock the first act came down, to acclamations of delight from the packed audience. In the wings Alexander was discussing with a new actor the recent burning down of Anderson's Theatre on Glasgow Green: 'They all, sir,' Alexander was saying, with his customary drawing of his fingers across his chin, 'they all, sir, come to the ground. No theatre seems exempt from fire but mine. I've been manager now for twenty years – '

Before he could finish, there came a murmur from out front. This grew louder and a cry of 'Fire!' was heard from the closely-packed upper gallery. Those elsewhere were in doubt as to whether the alarm was real. As the confusion increased, several gentlemen who were in the boxes rose and cried to those in the gallery, 'Keep your seats; there's no danger.' The band continued playing.

By this time the manager had come onstage. What he said was lost in the hubbub but it seems he had sent men up to the gallery to extinguish the flame. As he spoke a young man in a blue jacket put a foot over the front of the gallery and using his heel as a hammer, forced out the panel. There came a shout of 'It's the gas, it's the gas!' Smoke was seen, and a bright spark shot out. A man quietly took off his cap and extinguished the flame. Everything seemed righted. The audience settled down to see the remainder of the play.

At this point a fireman appeared in full uniform. At the sight of him there was a frantic rush to the main stair, which led to the street. Alexander roared himself hoarse in his efforts to subdue the panic. He rushed to the private door, followed by two of the Company, Mr Langley and Mr Fred Younge. Some stage carpenters joined them. The Fire Brigade, which had been summoned on the first alarm, then gone back thinking it was a false one, had by this time returned. Hatchets in hand they broke in the windows of the lane which looked on the staircase and entered. The crowd now made another dash forward towards the door, trampling one another. Those behind, hearing shrieks, pressed forward more strongly.

> Meanwhile Mr Alexander, Mr Langley and Mr Younge, clad in all the ghastly mockery of steel-clad warriors of the drama in which they had so lately been engaged, assisted by the carpenters, worked unceasingly to rescue the wretched sufferers. They never flagged in their efforts for an instant . . .

Seventy people had been trampled to death or suffocated. The experience and what he had seen haunted Alexander. The edge of his humour was blunted. He struggled on aimlessly, but the following year decided he could no longer battle with the attacks from the press and the public, and gave up the management of the theatre.

He slipped away, after a brief illness, on Monday 15th December 1851. That Friday, the day of his funeral, the Theatre Royal remained closed as a mark of respect. The *Glasgow Herald* proclaimed ambivalently:

> Mr Alexander's public character will be variously estimated. But we believe everyone will readily concede to him the character of an honest and industrious man, and an able member of his profession. Doubtless he had certain eccentricities, which were sometimes exhibited to the amusement of his audience, but these did not in any degree mar his general merits as an excellent performer . . .

Conceding that 'his performance as Dandie Dinmont in *Guy Mannering* more than once received commendations from Sir Walter Scott', the obituarist then stated bizarrely:

> [But of late] his low comedy has become rather broad rather

than humorous, and the short time he had for study forced him sometimes to interpolate words of his own in fault of those written by the author. Instead, however, of pursuing any further remarks of our own, we willingly give insertion to the following sketch, which we have reason to believe was written by Mr Alexander himself about the year 1834.

Occupying the remaining two-thirds of the space this lists dates and details up to that point, but reveals little of himself other than attributing the secret of his success 'to his *energy*'. It seems fitting that even here, he should have the last word. He is buried in the Glasgow Necropolis where an elaborate monument designed by an old employee, Thomas Dudgeon, marks his resting-place.

Lewis Chessmen

Knight

We are motionless in our display case:
not a tremor. Nothing new in that –
we have managed it down the ages.
Not always so, as you can imagine:
there were times it went hard with us,
but these were few and far between.
Our job always to protect our King
even if it meant sacrificing the Queen.
And each according to his station.
The Berserker may have been my junior
and not on horseback like myself,
both walrus-tusk Bishops seemingly frozen
in contemplation, but when it came
to the bit, we were a close-knit clan –
adept at adapting our battle-plan.
First in Scandinavia, then Lewis,
we were invincible. How many
black pieces have you come across?

Bishop

Nonsense, of course. He's no authority.
Typical of those who put hype
before scholarship. In the early days,
for the sake of distinction, sets were often
stained beetroot-red; this discharged,
in time, through the action of salt water.
Before that, references in Sanskrit
to passing the rainy season with 'not
warriors but green and yellow frogs
mottled with lac, leaping on garden-bed
squares'. Who'd have guessed it?
We might not have been here now:
the sailor who found us being slain
by a shepherd, who about to be hanged,
revealed the sand-bank where he'd
re-buried us. Potentially a worse fate
than being checkmated. Since then,
the Church has made many advances.

Queen

It is time women had a say.
Our day must come again:
the rules, though they remain
substantially the same,
be governed by female intuition,
not dominated by the rampant
cohorts of Church and State.
In real life, how many
get to the point of even
being mitred and gaitered –
and then generally too late.
Worst of all for the Queen,
who even if not taken
may see her side succumb
to an interminable equilibrium
of great powers: leaving her
no choice but share the fate
of her stale mate.

Berserker

I demand the last word. So many,
seeing my teeth embedded
in my shield, misconstrue me
as the epitome of battle-frenzy,
whereas they are quite mistaken.
What happened was, we were told
they wanted a line-up, as quickly
as we could make it: someone
was coming to date us. This
turned out to be not nearly
as exciting as it sounds. But
by the time we caught on,
it was too late. I'd already
had my fill of magic mushrooms.
What did they expect? Now please
avert your gaze: I am about
to discard my kit, and go bare sark.

Scenes of an Insomniac

As we grow older, it seems, we need less sleep. A bonus I find on long, insomnolent winter nights is the opportunity to recall moments in the theatre which have caught the imagination over the years. Mine stem from the '50s and '60s; the original tiny Traverse's stagings of work inaccessible (even in print) elsewhere; club-theatre productions of Miller and Tennessee Williams; Scofield and Bannen the precursors of a host of Hamlets from Stratford to Ledlanet; the shock-waves of *Look Back in Anger*; a vigorous diversity of regional voices where the RSC's RP had long been the norm; and the physicality and dynamism of Olivier in *Long Day's Journey Into Night* and as Archie Rice in *The Entertainer*. Early one morning my wife and I, waiting on the steps of the Old Vic for returns for Strindberg's *Dance of Death*, leaned aside to make way for a nondescript, bespectacled little figure in a grey raincoat. Only when he'd brushed past did we realise it was Olivier. That evening the spike-helmeted dance of the Boyars took us by storm, right at the back of the gods. At the interval, the usherette handing over our ice-creams had whispered throatily, 'Course, you know he's dyin' of cancer.'

Later and nearer home Albert Finney played Pirandello's crazed *Henry IV* at Glasgow Citizens'. The audience awaited his flamboyant first entrance – only to realise, when he spun away from a milling group of characters, that Finney had been on stage for some time without our being aware of it. For his pageant of *The Thrie Estaits* Guthrie contrived a spectacular version of this. As the rafters of the Assembly Hall rang to a fanfare of trumpets a host of courtiers strode in and formed a circle, their flag-poles meeting at the centre. These then parted like the petals of a huge flower, to reveal Divine Correctioun, spotlit and resplendent.

It can't be often that a character makes an impact after his final exit. Olivier's Shylock remained (for him) surprisingly muted as he departed defeated, for the last time. Then after a pause there came from the wings an animal howl of fury and pain. Another throat-catching moment outwith a play's formal action was at the first night of *A Day in the Death of Joe Egg*. We had witnessed the love and heartbreak of a mother and father for their grievously disabled daughter. At the interval the small girl playing the role reappeared and danced across the stage normally and happily. This glimpse of what the girl in the play might have been intensified our emotions, in an image that still lives with me.

The nearest I've been in to an audience literally rolling in the aisles (except there weren't any) was at the first night in the old Traverse, of John Byrne's *The Slab Boys*. The hilarity grew until folk were hanging on to one another, sucked into its hilarious thermals. Mercifully no one – then – fell from the seating modules, one of which later lost its back-strut. Vying with that as my funniest moment in the theatre must be a long-ago National Theatre version of *A Flea in her Ear*: As Feydeau's carousel of misunderstandings got into its hectic stride a Spanish nobleman's stutter returned as a result of someone swallowing the palate he had left in a glass of water.

What happens before the curtain rises or the cast appear can vary. For half an hour before Peter Brook's version of Seneca's *Oedipus*, a massive reflective cube revolved slowly, onstage. The beam of spotlights hitting it and angled into the auditorium soon reduced most of the audience to a state of trance. That and a giant phallus borne round the theatre, in a closing trad-jazz saturnalia, lent the play its nickname Box and Cox.

As a prelude to Howard Barker's *Vanya* a pinnie'd servant carried a tea-tray round a gallery, then tipped it and its contents over the rail, to clang on the stage. This was repeated until the scene was like a scrap-metal yard. I'm still trying to puzzle out the significance of the repeated gesture – other than as a symbol of oppressed domestics, everywhere. At the interval the wooden ice-cream spoons seemed to have run out and we were given metal ones. The friend sitting with my wife and myself wondered if we were meant to toss them down on the debris still littering the stage.

For C.P. Taylor's *Good* the Aldwych stage was open to the back wall and lit by a glare of white light, the musicians interweaving with the rest of the cast. Other companies mimicked this. But at the Tron they emerged from cupboard-like niches, effectively the compartments of Halder's mind. At the end he stands in Nazi uniform at the gates of Auschwitz, transfixed in his realisation that 'the music is real'. How would Michael Boyd achieve this? Doors opened at the side of the auditorium, through which a slanting light threw the musicians' shadows across the stage. This brought the play to an impeccably judged conclusion – and a shiver to the spine.

One of my most rewarding radio experiences was directing *Good*: for its human statement, its merging of Halder's internal and external worlds and his private and public roles; and for its depiction of the anguished threesome, himself, his wife and his dementing mother. For all the music in his head we used records which came across undisguisedly as such. But for the final scene I specially taped a group of musicians, with the same instrumentation as that of the concentration-camp band, playing a jaunty Schubert march. Played slightly off-key, its freshness and sound quality did give the necessary impression of 'liveness'.

Decades earlier, I'd directed Cecil's hilarious short play *Allergy* for Glasgow University Arts Theatre Group. And on many occasions we'd worked together in the radio studios. At the time of his cruelly sudden and early death he had suggested we see *Good* together, before its Aldwych run ended. Had the play been broadcast then it would have been impossible even on Radio 3 to fight successfully to keep the language so often vital to its rhythms and to reflecting the pressures within Halder's mind. In one particular scene this would have diminished the piece immeasurably. So artistically and for the play's integrity, the long wait was worth while. But we were constantly aware of the awful gulf of Cecil's absence. His warmth and humour, his loyalty to his friends and devotion to the theatre, and his untiring encouragement of other writers are still deeply missed by all who were close to him.

Another lingering image very different from that of Halder was also located on the rim of hell. At the end of Stephen MacDonald's open-stage production of *Crime and Punishment* in the Lyceum Little Theatre the horror of all that had happened in Raskolnikov's mind, and in reality, was held in the retina by a spiral staircase flooded with light the colour of blood. The power of suggestion, and with it the emotional impact, was heightened. I can still see its sheen, then its transference to white on the faces of the cast as they took their bow.

Curtain-calls can have their own piquancy. I wish I'd seen Wolfit milking the audience, ostensibly making to withdraw only to be drawn back and 'persuaded' to accept their whipped-up rapture. He was less ecstatically received on a return visit to Leeds. It seems he warned the cast in advance, 'They love me here: leave a pause for a round, before you cue me.' When he strode on, the silence was broken only by a carrying whisper from the gallery: 'Ye gods, Fookface is back!' The closest I witnessed to such old actor-manager bravura was when Andrew Cruickshank, stepping foot on the stage in *The Master Builder* after establishing his (latterly inescapable) Dr Cameron persona, stood an age, arms extended and cloaked like a Victorian Batman, awaiting (and activating) the old ladies' adulatory applause.

The most amazing call I've seen was by Marlene Dietrich: dragged on again and again by Burt Bacharach to blow kisses out front, each gesture and clutch at the piano seeming so spontaneous, it dumbfounded me to think that each night the routine was duplicated down to the flicker of an eyelash. This was a degree of professionalism-cum-showbiz which also took in the joyous but equally illusory 'impromptu' intimacy of Ella Fitzgerald.

After-show moments sometimes linger. I can still hear through the applause for *La Cantatrice Chauve*, in a tiny boulevard theatre in Paris, the rat-ta-tat of tip-up seats as a row of expressionless nuns trooped out like wax dolls, their faces expressionless. Fortuitous circumstance can add its own after-echoes – and mystery. One night at Toulon's Fort Napoleon eight Belgian actresses gave an entrancing open-air performance, part-dance and part-mime, of *Alice in Wonderland.* By mid-way the dew was so heavy they started slithering on the stage till one went barefoot – and the others followed suit. When the play had glissaded to its dreamlike conclusion they vanished, leaving only the moon's refractions and a filigree of drenched prints, where they had been.

Another all-woman touring troupe, from Mexico, almost raised the roof of the Assembly Rooms one Festival with *Donna Giovanni*, a stunning mix of *commedia*, cabaret and slapstick, and delicious *tableaux vivants*. Each visual moment sumptuously represented a famous painting. Less a scaled-down version of Mozart's opera than a flagrantly witty comment on it, the show ended with the Don in Death's icy (as against fiery) grip, naked figures intertwining in a baroque bacanal. Needless to say, the self-appointed arbiters of Edinburgh's morals were apoplectic.

A total unity was exquisitely provided by an Italian *Uncle Vanya,* on the 1996 official Festival. Set in a spacious glass cage it had the nurse place Vanya's flowers in a crystal vase. When he fired at the professor, the bullet shattered the vase, and the water poured out. Rather than a tricksy special effect, this was in tune with the production as a whole. At the end each 'he's gone' and 'they've gone', a perfectly timed and delivered grace note, contributed to the play's Chekhovian dying fall.

In the early '80s the Rustavelli Company hit our theatrical consciousness like a bombshell. During *The Caucasian Chalk Circle* a group of soldiers – soldiers, not thespians, as I'd never before seen – hurtled down the rake and almost into our laps: a reminder of Kenneth Tynan's shocked realisation during an earlier Russian company's tour that 'ten men on that stage could play Lear'. For the trial scene a man rushed on and without pause, draw two perfect circles in white chalk, on the forestage. Their *Richard III* was even more compelling, from the appearance of a humped figure in black – not Crookback but a narrating Queen Margaret – to its depiction of the princes in the tower and the working-out of the politics and drama of the piece, against a background of stygian forest one instant, dazzling mirrors the next.

I couldn't have been luckier in my years covering Edinburgh Festival drama for *The Listener.* In 1985 the Toho Company's absorption of *Macbeth* into Kabuki ritual was spellbinding. The 16th century Japanese setting cast a searing light on the play's psychology. From the first balletic appearance of the Witches to the sound of a great gong, the action gathered momentum with mesmeric clarity. The murder of Banquo and the banquet scene were viewed through a vast latticework. The production's silky beauty and spaciousness induced a filmic quality nowhere more telling than as Birnam Wood approached Dunsinane through the undulation of cherry-boughs, their whiteness sinister and presaging butchery.

Observing everything were two ancient crones, one on either side of the proscenium arch and placing the action in a Japanese cultural and religious context. At first dispassionate they grew, with ourselves, into numbed witnesses to atrocity. Imprinted on my memory are Banquo held upright by four horizontal samurai blades, crossed at his throat; Macbeth's face, stained with blood from his wife's hands after Duncan's murder; his poignant donning of her gown, after her suicide; and the ultimate slaying of the tyrant, and purging presentation of his head wrapped in white linen.

In its purity and sustained intensity, its marriage of image and music, and its overwhelming sadness, this for me remains the theatrical thrill of a lifetime.

Running it close was the Ninagawa Company's *Medea*, staged *al fresco* in the University of Edinburgh quad, with Mikijiro Hira again in the lead. One night they played in torrential rain. The elaborate costumes grew heavier, until his whirled cloak sent raindrops cascading from it, like a liquid catherine-wheel. No one who saw it will ever forget the elevation of Medea at the end, into the darkened sky. On our way home we passed the device used: a yellow cherry-picker (the slang name so apt), its huge arm hinged and black-draped. Not for an instant did this diminish the magic.

A sense of danger is one of the theatre's greatest thrills. This can be spuriously heightened. At one point in *I Hate Hamlet* a young soap-opera star booked to play the Prince in a provincial rep says 'I hate Hamlet'. There's a flash of lightning – and down the chimney comes the Ghost of John Barrymore (supposed to have once stayed in the house) to chastise him – and give him duelling lessons. During the Broadway run Nicol Williamson as Barrymore's Ghost, treating the young actor with increasing disdain, ended up piercing him with the sword. He walked out on the spot, leaving the management to recast the part. When I saw the show the replacement, apart from lacking the physique and emphatic heterosexuality demanded by the text, seemed to spend the entire evening skipping frantically out of poignard-range.

In London Williamson himself walked out on the audience early in a virtuoso performance of his own one-man play about Barrymore, which incorporated within the action a breath-taking (and demanding) series of voice exercises. For my wife and myself Williamson's reputation as a fiery brand long preceded this. I remember our settling to watch his Macbeth on television. Just as he embarked on his first soliloquy there was an acrid smell, and a wisp of smoke started spiralling from the back of the set. We never got to the dagger speech.

Crucial for good acting is not just good speaking, but good listening. In my own play *Thistlewood* in the Traverse, a scheming secretary-figure to Lord Sidmouth was played by Roy Marsden. I was very taken in one scene by how convincingly, in the few speeches he had, he gave the impression not just of coming in on cue but of weighing up all that was being said. In other words, of concentrated thought. When I told him this he explained that throughout the scene he was actually trying to learn next week's lines from a script on the lectern beside him.

The simplicity of many theatrical effects can be both striking and salutary. I recall the set being dismantled at the end of a Russian production of *A Month in the Country* – so touchingly and meaningfully it drew tears to the eyes. Think too of companies surviving on budgets a minute fraction of those who consider real leather, Swedish glass and Armani costumes the thing: the inventiveness and audacity of such wide-ranging groups as Paynes Plough and the old 7:84, Fifth Estate, Clyde Unity and Communicado.

The delight of the Actors Touring Company's *Don Quixote* was what they left to the imagination. Their windmills, actors birling ladders, were far more 'real' than in the techno-lavish National Theatre presentation, with Scofield hurtling down the aisle seemingly intent (as one review put it) on killing the stage electrician. As luck had it I saw only the first half of the ACT show: Quixote cracked a rib and the performance was abandoned at the interval.

On a later occasion I witnessed an even shorter extract, thanks to the untimely intervention of not so much a *deus* as a *diabolus ex machina*. My wife and I had gone to see a dramatisation of *Street of Crocodiles*. The lights came up on a set like a honeycomb, inhabited by surrealist creatures: a misshapen old man hobbling across the stage, bizarre bundles which might have been birds, and a disturbingly huge black cockroach. A human figure was climbing unsupported up one of the vertical walls. As this nightmarish Kafkan world unfolded there came a heavy thud, off. The action wavered a moment, then continued.

An SM announced: 'I'm sorry, ladies and gentlemen, but we'll have to stop. Please stay in your seats.' Consternation. Whispers, off. Then: 'Would you please leave the auditorium. And is there a doctor in the house?' As we filed out, the suave figure of a psychiatrist friend was ushered backstage. Soon a tannoy announcement apologised that there was no alternative but to cancel the show. It seemed (we learned later) that whoever should have been supporting a ladder in the wings wasn't, and someone had fallen and been injured. We hoped there might be tickets for one of the three remaining performances. But they were sold out.

Although I've since read the bizarre Bruno Schultz stories which were the basis for the play, I haven't the faintest notion how it might have developed. As it is, these abruptly truncated five minutes remain as gripping an opening to any play I've seen. Or rather, not seen. I expect I never will. At least on sleepless nights I can try to imagine whether the giant cockroach caught the man traversing the ceiling; or if he sprouted feathers and abseiled through the auditorium. As for the psychiatrist: did he really re-emerge or did he end up forever cocooned in the labyrinthine set? It certainly beats counting sheep.

By way of a postscript: two instances, both across the Pond, of remarks made by the person sitting next to me. One in the Lincoln Center. As my wife and I take our seats for *Six Degrees of Separation* I fold my jacket discreetly on my lap and sit back with, I feel, my elbows reasonably tucked in. No way. Close to my left ear comes a dry croak: '*You're encroaching!*' I draw into myself for fear of giving further offence. The evening is punctuated by sporadic sighs and tuttings, but no further castigations. Shortly before the end of the show the voice's shrivelled little owner gathers up two heaped armfuls of belongings and, like a bag-lady, rustles along the row to the side aisle, and away.

And last spring, sitting with a friend at the Guthrie Theater, Minneapolis. Watching Rita Dove's rich-textured version of the Oedipus story. A plantation-owner's wife has borne a child to one of her overweening husband's black slaves. Sold off at birth, and his death planned, he returns (inevitably) twenty years later. As tension heightens the man next to me, unaccompanied and totally engrossed, carries on a running commentary. Aimed not at me but at the actors, or rather the characters, on stage. *Sotto* at first, but increasingly exasperated and uninhibited as the story progresses. Until near the end he responds to the central character's desperate plea 'Who is my father, I must know' with a growled 'You oughta, you just *killed* him.' Finally Oedipus's heartrending 'Who is my mother?' elicits a stupefied: 'Gawdsakes man, you're *lookin'* at her!'

Walking on Water

FROM AN ADDRESS TO THE FRIENDS OF CLEVELAND
PLAY HOUSE, OHIO, JAN. 1991

The prospect of addressing you this evening gave me butterflies in my stomach, which tend to assail me before any social event – all the more on unfamiliar territory or when I sense I am, as here, heavily outgunned. So thank you for the warmth of your welcome – and for being so ease-putting. I can even remember the injunctions I took care to jot down on my cuff beforehand: one, don't gabble; and two, keep off the sauce.

I don't know if these reflect on me or on my Scottishness. If the latter I hope I may give the lie to national stereotyping – not least by way of reciprocation: all the Americans I've met have been courteous, cultured and (well almost all) unassuming and introvert. You have of course your vastly varied States. Hearing that my first touch-down on this side of the Water would be in Ohio, friends said I was in for a shock. Most of my preconceptions have already been demolished: not least those based on Les Roberts's thriller *Full Cleveland,* set in 'the premier city of Lake Erie – where money, the mob and revenge rule'. The flight from New York offered a different perspective: two businessmen from the Big Apple running down the mid-West. It was rather like being on the shuttle back home, with a pair of London sophisticates sounding off about Scotland.

On the transatlantic leg I'd chuckled at Helene Hanff's *Underfoot in Show Business*. She gives a delicious account of a new musical show *Away We Go* which toured catastrophically and bombed at New Haven where, although it still wasn't ready for the critics, one sneaked a preview and wired his office 'NO LEGS NO JOKES NO CHANCE'. With not enough notice for its Broadway run to be cancelled the vultures were hovering. But rewritten, with a new musical score and retitled *Oklahoma!* (complete with exclamation-point) it became a huge hit. Hanff cites this as an extreme instance of what she names Flanagan's Law – 'the only predictable thing about the Theatre is its *un*predictability.'

In 1984 I was awarded a travel scholarship stipulating South Africa, a place I'd never have dreamed of visiting otherwise. This led to a play *By the Pool*, set in a suburb of Johannesburg. Three years ago, against the odds, it was premiered on the Edinburgh Festival Fringe. In the audience one day were two subscribers from Cleveland Play House. Afterwards they wrote urging the Theatre to stage it. (If that excellent couple aren't here this evening, I hope I'll be able to meet and thank them at some point during my stay.) Nine times out of ten such a letter would be filed and forgotten. Instead the literary manager wrote asking for a script. Ninety-nine times in a hundred nothing would have come of this. But it was passed to your artistic director Josie Abady, who determined to direct it. The board agreed. Now it's in rehearsal: a clear case of Flanagan's Law in action.

So how does it feel, being here? I'm completely bowled over by Philip Johnson's 'stately pleasure-dome' of a theatre, its modules and minarets so dramatic in their surroundings; and by the interior with its gleaming tiled walkways and glass walls. What really impresses me though, is the support not just Theatre but the Arts in general receive from individuals and groups like yourselves, through your tireless support and fundraising activities. I gasp at the extent of private and corporate sponsorship of the Arts. There are individual parallels between Edinburgh's Usher and McEwan Halls, founded by big brewers, and the Cleveland Orchestra's Conservation Hall, built through a wealthy and public-spirited family. But the massive scale of support – equally evident in your invitingly airy and spacious Art Gallery and its collection – is astounding.

All I miss are exercise and fresh-air: I've been warned not to walk through the snow as I'd prefer, but always to take a cab to my skyscraper hotel. The one time I ventured abroad confirmed (luckily without mishap) how radically things can change within one block, or at an intersection. As for the hotel, I couldn't be comfier. Just one thing was disconcerting. Keen to blend in I'd say 'Have a nice day' to anyone I met in the elevator. This was met by grim glares. Then it clicked. It was after all the Clinic Center Hotel: these were the families of transplant patients. Now I keep my head down as they glide past, white-clad sheiks and their entourages among them, silent and ashen-faced.

I don't know how many of you may be Daughters of the Revolution. Josie, although not one by birthright, certainly displays the more commendable strengths (and no sign of what may be the dubious downside) of the breed. Since my arrival she has shown determination, tact, imaginative insight and total commitment to the work on hand. Nor does her dynamism appear to brush others aside, or inhibit her staff – I've already come across characters colourful and expressive enough to have stepped out of Damon Runyan.

Rehearsals are proving a voyage of discovery. The casting impeccable. And providing nice moments. One of my characters speaks of another as moving 'like a young gazelle'. Angela Thornton who plays her told me (eyes glistening) that when she worked for Noel Coward, he described her in those very words. David Potts's set-model with something of the warmth and boldness of Hockney in its colour-scheme is striking. My one worry had been that the *pool* of the play's title, which is central to the action, might for practical purposes have to be cheated into the wings. But no: enhanced by subtle reflections from Richard Winkler's lighting design, it will be dramatically centre-stage (the benefit of having a redoubtable Opera man to hand).

In the meantime we're making do with its outline, marked in blue tape on the rehearsal-room floor. I observe from a discreet distance as the characters walk carefully round it, or stand by its rim. Only Josie ignores and constantly crosses the demarcation line. This augurs well. I've been very lucky in the directors I've worked with previously. But Josie is the first I've come across, who can walk on water.

Granite Sculptor
RONALD RAE

Stephen Leacock wrote, as I remember it, of a cowboy drinking in a saloon who suddenly threw himself off his bar stool, threw himself out of the swing doors, threw himself on to his horse and rode madly off in all directions. I can imagine Ronald Rae doing just that. To describe him as a remarkable man would be a ludicrous understatement. He gives the impression of being several men, and energies, rolled into one lithe frame topped by an exuberant coup of curly dark hair. His generous beard is not merely an appendage but an expressive feature in itself, especially when he is in full conversational flood – which is often. He is no more a man for a sound-bite than for doing things by halves. When he decided to become a sculptor he took on a lifetime's burden of responsibility to himself and his art, and to tapping internal and external forces and putting them at the disposal of the demon within. Unlike Leacock's cowboy he focuses these and his own physical strength single-mindedly on the task on hand.

Ronald Rae was born in Ayr in 1946 and went to primary school down the road from Burns's cottage in Alloway. At fourteen he made his first sculpture in granite, one of the hardest stones in the world. It was the start of an obsession. In 1965 he attended sculpture classes at Glasgow School of Art where I suspect attempts were made to impose on him other curricular activities which he found distracting or inhibiting. Three years later he became a fulltime student at Edinburgh College of Art. Again though, as the foreward to a catalogue of his work explains: 'unable to constrain his own creative drive within a college timetable, he left after one year to continue his own artistic development'.

This he has done over the years with a fervour that would have broken anyone less strong in himself, and less dedicated. At times it has been a close-run thing. The physical and mental disciplines he imposes on himself are rigorous. For a start and though tackling blocks of granite on a monumental scale he has consistently shunned the use of electric or mechanical tools: everything is hand-chiselled, shaped by the sweat of his brow, a driving will, and the strength of his arm. Nor in emotional and psychological terms is his subject-matter an easy option. He is inspired by literature, loves poetry and finds himself deeply moved by the tragedies of life. His themes are universal, his works capable of inspiring extraordinary depth of feeling – and pity.

Such responses are also summoned up by his drawings, of which I first really became aware in an exhibition in Edinburgh's 369 Gallery in the 1980s. They were painful depictions of down-and-outs in the Grassmarket which in seemingly simple lines caught something of the degradation of the derelicts and the squalor of their surroundings, while investing them with a pathos emanating from the artist's own intense humanity. This was long before such studies became the fashion.

We also have a close friend who owns one of Ronald's sheep drawings: as sheepish a sheep as you'd hope to see. When my BBC colleagues asked me to choose a departure present I decided on something by Ronald. He took me to where he had his store. They filled an attic in their hundreds . . . studies in pencil, pen-and-ink, and charcoal. Many had been exhibited. More await their turn. Others had already gone to public and private collections throughout the world.

The choice wasn't easy. But eventually it was a sheep – rather than one of the more harrowing ones – I decided on. Drawn with satisfying clarity of line, it is in simple black on white apart from a pink blob of colour, and has an ambiguous head-down posture: to look at it you couldn't be quite sure whether it is about to nibble a clump of juicy grass, or has its wicked eye on you and is on the point of butting you up the bum.

The presentation took place at my farewell dinner in the boardroom of the BBC's Edinburgh premises. On the wall there is a portrait of the Queen. I'm told it was by the narrowest of shaves that I ended up back home with my sheep, and Her Majesty still on the wall – rather than vice versa. I still occasionally shudder at what the consequences might have been.

But back to Ronald Rae. He has had many other drawings on show, including a group on religious themes in the Netherbow Arts Centre; and in Glasgow's Compass Gallery, disturbing figures who seemed not merely overshadowed by but somehow invested, often through heavy cross-hatching, with a darkness of the soul, an overwhelming angst or guilt of some kind. I've also seen in his sketchpads tiny jewel-like drawings of figures, some with splashes of colour, that had the lucidity of children's book-illustrations or theatrical costume-designs in miniature.

His sculptures in contrast are on such a scale – starting with stones weighing many tons – that a single work can occupy him for months, even years. This is certainly true of the works with which he established his reputation. His 1979 *Golgotha Madonna,* of Cornish granite, a metre and a half high and one of five studies depicting the 'Tragic Sacrifice of Christ', is in Rozelle Park in Ayr. *Return of the Prodigal* (1983), twice as big, depicts a male figure taking his son to his breast with a tenderness that belies the massiveness of the structure and rough texture of the stone. Sited at the headquarters of General Accident (now CGU) in Perth this was Rae's touching interpretation of the Company's motto, 'I warn and I protect'.

The religious strand running through his work is confirmed by other titles such as *Man of Sorrows, John the Baptist, Gethsemane* and *Lazarus.* A wider humanity is suggested by *Famine* and *Hiroshima Departed.* There are poignant studies of a cow elephant with her trunk round a baby (1987) and later *Wounded Elephant* (1990–91). Since 1998 have come *Animals in a War Memorial, Bear* and *Calf.*

This conveys his thematic and emotional spectrum. He is no dilettante fancier of pretty patterns or superficial statements. In an astonishing mix of the physical and the spiritual, he gets to what he believes to be the heart of things. No surprise that this is demanding – and draining. Or that those who admire him do so intensely.

It is breathtaking to see him at work. There is a film of him carving outside Dunfermline College, Cramond. He speaks to camera, describes in rational tones what he intends, explains something of his aesthetic. Then his syntactic units become more staccato, more explosive, as he tugs down his protective visor and starts chiselling in such bursts of energy you'd think the film had been speeded up. He goes at it – I'm sure he would accord with this – like a man possessed. Then stops, examines what he has done. Raising the visor, he gasps for air. He may stand and study the work-in-progress. Or splash a bucket of water over it to see how the light strikes the stone. Standing back to survey it and perhaps cry, 'My God, it's gone all wrong . . . How could it possibly have turned out like that?'

Then he'll turn and explain how frightened he is that a particular piece may break off. If it does, months of labour could be undone. On the other hand, it is often as if something guides even that, and the consequent fault-line can be put to advantage. The perfect activity for a manic depressive I suppose; bursts of frenetic and demanding hammering, followed by imposed stasis, giving knotted muscles time to recover for the next bout . . .

After the film made by Steve and Carolyn Horn was edited it was offered to BBC Scotland. This was at the time when a quota of work from Independents was being introduced. The response was to ask whether their hope was that the existing film might be shown, or for the BBC to remake their own version. When told the former, it was offhandedly returned. I suspect what hadn't been taken into account was the number of man hours that would have been needed, to replicate even the shortened film given Ronald's work-method and the long pauses while he waited for inspiration to strike – then would leap frenziedly into action. In budgeting terms it would have been rather akin to one of those Disney accounts of flowers leafing and budding. Anyway, it went out eventually on BBC2 – in a 10x10 slot, under its own steam.

There is a profound spirituality in Ronald Rae as well as in his work. The one imbues the other. This does not mean there won't be a string of profanities if things go wrong. Or if the hammer slips on the chisel. Not long back, he badly damaged his thumb. There are also, as the years slip by, the aches and agues caused by having to lie prone or sit in the one position, to tackle a particular part – say the underside – of the stone.

What registers as forcefully as his dynamism – again the two go hand in hand – is how much he cares. In conversation he keeps reiterating this, as though it could be in any doubt. He cares deeply about his craft, about each sculpture, about the pain and vulnerability of humankind to which so much of his work gives expression. He is of the world, yet in a way totally unworldly.

One day he was approached by a Rory Bremner who indicated that he admired his work. Both seemed to take to one another, and an animated conversation ensued. Ronald waxed lyrical – at unconstrained length, I've no doubt – about his sculpture. Then paused and said, 'Tell me Rory, what is it you do yourself then?'

In the wake of their meeting came a contribution to another television programme in which Rory Bremner enthused about the sculptures. Ronald is a gift as a performer – simply because he isn't performing at all, but being totally himself. That's to say, he is larger than life to start with. And fires on all cylinders. His partner Pauline MacDonald, herself a talented textile artist dedicated to being his secretary, PR officer and fulltime walker-on-eggs and support system, had the idea of proposing him for Radio 3's 'Private Passions' series. In due course he was vetted and flown down to London for the interview. His love of music came across, as did his verve for living. His sheer passion. With musical illustrations ranging from Schubert to Shostakovitch.

This is where we come to the hard bit. The name Ronald Rae does not appear in the catalogues of those Galleries one would hope might have by now expressed an interest in him. It is not that his work hasn't been drawn to their attention. Pauline is tirelessly assiduous on his behalf. There have been approving articles in journals. He has an intense band of admirers. What I find particularly surprising (and must be hurtful to him) is the total blackout on his sculpture to date by the Scottish National Gallery of Modern Art – itself no more than a stone's throw from where for a while he had his workyard.

Not only that: the Gallery bookshop will not even entertain the catalogue of his major works. It seems they are 'too sentimental . . . too populist'. Is this the price of being representational in an age when art has moved beyond that? Of lacking the shock value necessary to be taken up by the market-force driven (and driving) Charles Saatchi? The sophistication to be trendy? Does it boil down to some equivalent of the castigation of James MacMillan by those jaundiced reviewers who find him too accessible, too tuneful? Or simply that Rae does not move in the right circles?

It is especially dispiriting in that the large lawn round the Gallery would be perfect for work of such a scale to respond to the vagaries of the weather and play of changing light. Even more ironically just over the road, in front of the Dean Gallery now given over to Paolozzi's more cerebral hardware, is another grassy stretch which would be equally fitting.

Against this there has been meaningful recognition elsewhere. Since 1987 Witley Court, near Worcester, has been in the care of English Heritage. In an imaginative partnership with the Jerwood Foundation a sculpture park has been installed in the grounds, with a view to establishing a permanent collection. The first seven purchases towards this have been made: included are works by Elizabeth Frink, Michael Ayrton, Anthony Gormley – and Ronald Rae. An arts feature in *The Telegraph*, praising the initiative, pointed out how much more easily visiting families can relate to sculptures in a garden than in a gallery: 'It is delightful to hear children's comments – on Ronald Rae's wrinkled grieving *Widow Woman*, for example: "The woman with a nice face"; and on a Frink figure, "It's a troll!" '

Consistent with this, in May 1999 an exhibition of Rae's sculptures was installed in a section of London's Regent's Park. Transporting them there was virtually a military operation. But the difficulties and a concern to position the pieces aesthetically were rewarded by a groundswell of public enthusiasm. Many people have written to the sculptor not just to say they 'like' or 'admire' this or that work but to express their *feelings* towards them and stress how strongly they relate to them. Local residents have echoed this. One who walks through the park to work enthused in the *Camden Journal:* 'Nothing lifts my spirits more than to appreciate these extraordinary shapes – contorting, twisting, turning, depicting every human and animal condition. They delight both young and old. Why can't they remain permanently in Regent's Park where the zoomorphic relationship between these magnificent forms adapts harmoniously in natural surroundings?'

On my last visit one sculpture was being photographed, while another had round it a group of tourists eyeing it and caressing its surfaces.

Here things take an odd twist. The Lords Hansard for 8th Nov. 1999 reports on a debate on Royal Parks. Declaring 'an interest . . . as a joint trustee of the Royal Parks Appeal of H.R.H. the Prince of Wales' Lord St John of Fawsley cavilled at the intrusion of a flower-show, theatrical performances and by implication increased public intrusion on his sacred preserve. He went on:

> A creeping commercialism is taking root. Let us take the example of Ronald Rae. I have nothing against Mr Rae, and indeed I do not know him. Until his work suddenly landed in the middle of the park, I had never seen it. Twenty huge works suddenly arrived in the Nesfield gardens . . . In a space of less than nine acres, the twenty huge sculptures were dumped for sale, for the benefit of Mr Rae. I rang up Camden Council, which had not even given planning permission. When I inquired, their representatives said that a different department

was responsible. They admitted that an error had been made but said they would grant permission retrospectively. One can imagine the fate of someone who produced that excuse in relation to a house. Will the Minister tell the House when the sculptures are going to be removed?

Had he on his foppish meanderings stubbed his delicate toes on them? If so I suppose it's a mercy he didn't dance around shrieking 'Off with their heads!' While he is entitled to his elitist viewpoint I deplore his disdainful reference to the sculptor who has no means of redress. The carvings were installed in good faith after long-term and what were believed to be proper negotiations, in the hope that they would give joy to others in what was seen as an ideal natural environment. For the sculptor any sale would be a welcome bonus. But the attribution of some calculated marketing motive, compounded by the use of the term 'dumped', is both offensive and mean-spirited.

It seemed Fawsley's attempt to be the sole arbiter of public taste had fallen on barren soil. But a year on, after a further complaint from him that they were still 'disfiguring' his park, Lord McIntosh of Haringey announced (Hansard 24th Oct. 2000) that 'the statues will be removed by March of next year and that area will be returned to parkland'. This threat, with the foot and mouth restrictions a dominant factor, did not materialise. But there is no denying the trepidation with which Ronald Rae and Pauline MacDonlad awaited developments. On the one hand there was their concern over the logistic and economic implications: where could the sculptures go and who would foot the bill? And on the other the deeper impact on Ronald himself, who could at times see no way forward in his art: the outcome of four decades of total dedication to the urgings of his inner voice.

It can only be hoped his spirit has not been damped by recurring rebuffs, but that the strike of his chisel will continue to be the song of a man who has come through; who in carving the most beautiful stone he knows, not only identifies with and strengthens his Celtic roots but hopes to make a personal statement that will, in Pauline MacDonald's words, 'withstand the rigours of time to communicate his universal themes to the generations of the future'.

Since the above was written there has been an extension of tenure for the sculptures in Regent's Park. Despite the fulminations of Lord Foppingham, the tide seems at last to be turning in their favour. *Gethsemane* has been bought be a private collector in the U.K. A large *Elephant and Calf* has gone to an American buyer and will be shipped out to Millbrook, New York, at the end of the exhibition. Crucially, the Yorkshre Sculpture Park hopes to find funding for a major display of Rae's work in May 2002: this to include all the Regent's Park pieces and one of his latest sculptures, a magnificent sixteen-ton *Tyger Tyger* currently at the Natural History Museum. Larger than life, couchant and in relief, it is fluidly worked into the stone and so at peace it could be slumbering were it not for the watchful eyes. As the title suggests, it is in a way a homage to William Blake. A thing of beauty, from a man himself a visionary.

Ronald Rae views adversity not bitterly but with a concern lest his work and his commitment to it may be undermined. Hurts are seen not as blows to his ego but to his whole *raison d'être*. Revisiting the Maclaurin Art Gallery in Ayr he is aware of the graffiti and broken bottles littered round his sculptures, but accepts these because he can see beyond them to what he regards as the destiny of the pieces themselves. The products of his own vision. So he will again set off to Royal Deeside in search of granite for his next sculpture. Increasingly, as he puts it, and as time goes by, *'to sing and celebrate this little passage between birth and death'*.

Blossom Time

Dear Rosie,

Sorry haven't written sooner. So much scurrying around, we've lost all notion of time. Many congrats on doing so well: agree due a break. Cubbyhole at your disposal whenever. But maybe better prospects. Read on! We've begun flat-hunt. Saw one today. Clevedon Rd. Outer hall with positively Clytemnestra-type pillars. Inner hall: Regency stripes. Could never take it: our Mrs Chatter-on would go demented. While we were looking, bell went and in swanned Couple A. Minutes later, second couple: flown-the-coop Hubbie of Wife A plus new Bidey-in. Measuring tapes at 20 paces. Bell again. Couple C: spring-rusty Glesca Soap Star + same-sex Partner. Much Hyndland banter. By now caretaker shaking in shoes: clearly suspects Trojan Horse plot. Next: Prof D plus wife. Again *tutti* known to *tutti*. We fled.

On way out, noticed crack from outer hall cupola to cornice level. Just bomb-damage, said caretaker: it settled long ago. Nuff said. Alongside our rusty bikes: a split-new Volvo and the Prof's white Merc. Guess who won't be getting the flat. Not to worry. Still looking. Let you know a.s.a.p.

Love, S.

Dear Rosie,
Hasty note. Ta for yours. Yes, sooner the better. Still no joy, flat-wise. But no panic. So long as you don't mind sharing cubby-hole with the cat (only joking!). Blossom-time: does the soul good. I often marvel at what a cherry-orchard must look like. Before they chop it down, that is . . .
    Love S.
    PS: Just seen one in today's *Herald*: sounds perfect.

Dear Rosie,
Have viewed it. Bottom half of divided villa. View across Bots, ergo no fear of being built on/overlooked. Big lawn plus fruit-trees. Owner a bit wan. But tactfully left us to look round. Odd thing. In main bedroom (J. hates <u>master</u>): antique dressing-table with mirror sections. From one angle they reflected pear and apple blossom in the garden. White and pink. Swaying in the breeze. Suddenly could've sworn I saw a woman's face reflected. Spun round, but of course nothing. Asked J. to sit there, to see if she noticed anything. Not a dicky. So shrugged it off. Anyway, price seems okay. If no hols and we keep off the vino for next ten years. Going back at weekend with tape-measure. Cross fingers plus light joss-sticks for us. Will let you know.
    Love, S.

Dear Rosie,
We've both taken to it even more, second time round. Every aspect. Rooms so spacious. Your bedroom overlooks garden. Owner (chap called A. McL——, friendly if a bit sombre) says he'll be leaving curtains (huge – could double as house-tabs) and carpets (ditto): an absolute godsend, as none of ours'd come near. Also maybe a few items of furniture, as seems he's moving to something smaller. Oh: J. said she felt something odd in bedroom this time – as if someone outside window. But when she turned round, no one there. What d'you expect, I said, we're two floors up. Still maybe we'll hear romantic swish of crinolines across upper landing floorboards at night! Mind the Goldoni (was it Marivaux?) at the Citz . . . Survey pends.
    Love, S.

Dear Rosie,
Hey there. Got it! All bar the scrawls on the dotted line. Bubbly on ice.
  Love and toodle-pip. S.

Dear Rosie,
Deal's off. Seems another offer at the last second. J. tearing her hair. No
wonder. She'd every nook and cranny worked out. Not to mention the
garden. The one mercy, ours not yet on market. More I think about it the
more I resent being led up garden path. Sent whey-face a real stinker saying
how betrayed we feel. And hoping he's proud of himself. Looks like you'll
be stuck with cubby-hole again. Sorry in triplicate. But hope see you soon
for aw that.
  Love, S.

Dear Rosie,
Just a 2-liner. After what I said in last letter, thought I ought to send the
attached. Feel a real heel. Poor sod. But how were we to . . . dot, dot, dot?
  Love, S.

  [enclosed]

Dear Mr C—,
I appreciate how you feel. But the other offer was so extravagantly above the
asking-price my solicitor couldn't refuse. People returning from abroad it seems,
and desperate. At least you weren't beaten by a hairsbreadth. Or drawn into a
costly auction. On a personal note. I took to you both when you came to see the
flat. And wouldn't have wanted to cast a shadow over you, even inadvertantly.
Last year our younger daughter had a break-down. And in the autumn took
her life. Without elaborating, she was found in the garden. I don't know the
effect of this if you'd found out after moving in, or from other sources. Especially
as her Christian name was the same as your wife's. So all may be for the best.
At any rate I hope you see it in that light, and won't remain aggrieved.
  Kind regards.
  A—— McL——

Summer People

One morning in early November 1998 Anna Crowe and I were collected by car from a hotel in central Barcelona. A third passenger was poet and critic Jaume Perez i Montaner, then a teacher at València University. Driving was Francesc Parcerisas, the respected director of the Institució de les Lletres Catalanes. He turned right into the Ramblas with their arched plane-trees, their stacked bird-cages and floral displays, past the Boqueria Market then the shrouded Liceu Opera House, still undergoing restoration after the second disastrous fire in its history.

Near the waterfront and under the gaze of Columbus on his pillar we drew up at the Departament de Cultura to take on board a stack of English-Catalan dictionaries and thesauruses. Then with two other cars we headed out of the city. Soon the jagged outline of Montserrat loomed through the haze. Passing closer we could make out one vast boulder supporting a smaller one, like a hunched bird of prey. The massif diminished behind us as we sped north, skirting reservoir after reservoir, the road spiralling into the mountains.

That August I'd received a phone-call from Francesc Parserisas, in Edinburgh to read at a *Catalonia/Caledonia* event in the Scottish Poetry Library. He wanted to know if I'd take part in a translation seminar 'in an austere mountain setting'. Regretfully I said I spoke neither Spanish nor Catalan. He assured me this wouldn't be necessary: my task would simply be to offer guidance on the 'nuances' of my poetry. We met briefly and he went into fuller detail. Four concentrated days would be spent with another writer and a team of translators in the mediaeval village of Farrera de Pallars, 4,000 feet up in the Catalan Pyrenees. No further arm-twisting was needed. A formal invitation followed. Anna Crowe was also invited.

On the flight out I relished her Peterloo volume *Skating out of the House*. Her poems, elegantly crafted and rich in cultural allusion, draw perceptively on music and painting and reveal a wide and deep knowledge of the natural world. On the Iberian Airways leg from Heathrow the full moon seemed for a spell borne on the plane's port wing-tip like a treasure-hoard. Francesc was waiting for me in Barcelona's huge glass-cube terminal building. Outside my hotel was a statue of the 19th century painter Marià Fortuny after whom the street is named. The bar-restaurant was shut. When I asked if there was anywhere I could get a coffee, the night-porter gestured grandiosely towards the teeming café-world outside.

Waking at six the next morning I peered out at tiered apartment blocks with ricketty staircases. On the balcony opposite it seemed a misshapen dwarf had his eyes trained on me. It was too dark to see properly so I went back to bed, somewhat disconcerted. An hour or so later it was light enough to make out a giant teddy-bear hung out to dry, alongside the bed-sheets.

Rounding hairpin upon hairpin we passed signs to the Fountain of the Horse and the Palace of the Walnut Trees and after three hours came to Farrera, huddled round the 17th century bell-tower of Sant Roc, overlooking the Coma de Burg valley, with the snow-capped peaks of Andorra beyond. In the face of the region's dwindling population and mindful of the beauty of the surrounding countryside a number of the village's buildings, including the former school, have been attractively renovated to form the Centre d'Art i Natura. Wild flower and chamois – and translator – country par excellence.

Non-profitmaking and part-funded by the European Commission for Cultural Action, the Centre enjoys close links with other countries. Initially it was visited mainly by geographers, but shortly before our arrival there had been a successful symposium for composers and astronomers. A big barn built into the rock-face is earmarked for a display area complete with a printing-press. Shades of Patrick Geddes's Scots College at Montpellier spring to mind.

We were shown to our rooms in three houses adjoining that of the Centre's Director Lluís Llobt and his wife Cesca, at whose hospitable table we would eat: their mouth-watering meals aromatically herbed and accompanied by red and white wines; whisky, brandy and the sweetest of Muscadets passed round with the coffee.

The plan was for Francesc and his assistant Iolanda Pelegrí each to work with one poet and four other translators. Of these Miquel Desclot has in print translations from Italian, French, Japanese and English and was in the process of 'reclaiming Petrarch for Catalan'. Didac Pujol's subjects include John Burnside and Seamus Heaney; while Dolors Udina has under her belt an extensive range of novelists from Toni Morrison to Nadine Gordimer and J.M. Coetzee. Further subjects among the group – almost all of them academics – included William Carlos Williams, Sylvia Plath, the adventures of *Asterix* and the screenplay of *Pulp Fiction*.

My poem-sequence *The Luncheon of the Boating Party* comprises a series of monologues spoken by figures in Renoir's famous painting and by the artist himself, recalling those days at Chatou. First came a literal translation, the group tackling a section (or voice) each. Then followed minute discussion, the dictionaries in constant use. Further renderings led to the emergence of *El dinar dels barquers* (as against the Spanish *Almuerzo de remeros*). My main job was to clarify the sense and convey any undercurrents, and with Catalan much less rich in synonyms than English, to offer alternatives. Some were felt out of place: for 'snotty bitch' (glossed as 'lady muck') I was sorry finally to lose the graphic 'queen of the artichoke field'.

The gerund being unlike English, syntax was constantly reworked. And with no direct parallel to the line-breaks and rhyme-schemes underpinning the original, alternative patterns and correspondences had to be sought. As to punctuation: for a question that didn't open with an interrogative or was contained in a longer sentence, an inverted question-mark or open-query sign would be inserted: something Catalan purists still resist, given its Castilian origin.

That night and the next I lay awake, the local dogs howling like a pack of word-wolves, fangs at the ready. I wondered if there'd come a time when no nuances might be good nuances. Halfway, Anna and I switched groups. With me the process became more of a communal one. What still most excited me was the emergence, evident when read aloud, of the Catalan cadences – the poems' new *music*. I'd have liked to compare versions from each translator: as it was I marvelled at the harmony of their discussions.

On a lunch-time walk to an old chapel across the horseshoe-shaped valley we pondered the ideal collective term for our team of translators. The one eventually hit on, a *confluence*, seems just right: each a tributary, feeding the main current. Behind the chapel's studded main door was a bird's nest. And our track back down the slope from the sun-bleached building was through a ring of tangled bushes laden with gleaming rose-hips.

On the last evening work pursued us to the dinner-table. Botanical tomes were produced so that marsh marigold, meadow-sweet and other flowers in Anna's poems could be double-checked and verified in Latin. After the meal came readings; and much Muscadet. No dogs that night. But chill setting in. Just before dawn, with shadow receding across the valley like a dark wing, I headed for the tree-line. The final slope wasn't unscaleable but thicketed, with a coating of frost: no saying how treacherous it might soon become. A twisted ankle was the last thing I wanted. The cleanness of the air, the total silence and the autumn colours intensifying by the minute were exhilarating. Then a scramble back for coffee, a hasty shower, and the final session.

With animated discussions on rhyme-patterns lingering in the ear I was intrigued to find, in Robert Hughes's superb *Barcelona*, this observation from 'Les Flors del Gay Saber', a treatise on mediaeval Provençal usage: '"*Li catala son grand dictayre Pero d'aysso no sabon gayre car de petit fan plenier so . . .* ", meaning roughly that the Catalans are fine poets, full of inspiration, but not technically good, because they are always mixing up open and closed vowels.'

Before leaving, our group posed for a final array of cameras then stood aside as some cattle, one with a sonorous bell, swayed down the track. The gnarled old farmer with them responded to our greeting, his gruff *'Good day, summer people'* a wry reminder of our impermanency and that it was time to head back to the city. This time by a different route: the red sun setting behind the mountain spine, then enveloping darkness; miles of motorway descent, the glow of the city eventually emerging.

It is tempting to look for parallels between Catalan and Scots. Wise though to *ca canny.* Three hundred years ago Felipe V banned the ancestral tongue he identified with separatist aspirations. After 1939 Franco, revoking the statute of autonomy which seven years earlier had officially recognised Catalan alongside Castilian, adopted a similar policy and outlawed the language. Theatre performances were banned until 1946. Despite a later relaxing of the ban it was not until two years after Franco's death in 1975 that the founding of the Associació d'Escriptors en Llengua Catalana and the re-launch of the Centre Català del PEN Club defended the role of the writer and the promotion of Catalan literature. Laws passed in 1979 and 1983 again gave linguistic autonomy to Catalonia, ensuring that public use of the tongue was not penalised.

In standardising Catalan the engineer-linguist Pompeu Fabra (1868–1948) chose those elements of vocabulary and syntax which most differed from the traditionally dominant Castilian. Nonetheless Fabra took care, as an expert on Catalan has put it (contrast the formal attempts to reinstate Lallans), to provide 'an intellectual register, either by borrowing from the languages of Europe's major cultures, or by exploiting the native resources of his own language, so that Catalan would formally be suitable for use in all areas of social activity, including the highest levels of culture and scientific investigation'.

In its various dialect forms Catalan is today spoken by some seven million people, in Valencia, Andorra and the Balearics as well as in Catalonia. For a considerable time there has been a growing move to make it the only language to be used officially. Again whereas we take for granted that any anthology of current Scottish writing will be predominantly in English, however 'tipped with Scots', nothing in high Spanish – even by a writer born and living in Catalonia – is classified as Catalan literature.

Shortly after our Farrera week Francesc Parserisas was to attend a conference in Wales, on 'peripheral languages'. On such occasions reciprocal translation is strongly advocated. Ideally this surmounts barriers and furthers mutual understanding. I suspect too that, between a Catalan and a Gael for instance, there must be shared empathies and perceptions. At Farrera itself subsequent seminars have embraced Breton and Hebrew, again in the hope of reciprocation. At the same time and satisfying though this may be for the Catalan writer, the potential increase in his or her readership remains tightly circumscribed.

What then of English, more globally dominant than ever? Counter to general assumption relatively little foreign poetry is in fact these days translated into English – and even less gets published. I am told for instance that there is a much wider range of modern Russian poetry available in Italian than there is in English. And although comprehensive anthologies of modern Catalan poetry exist in Italian and Croatian, none is (to my knowledge) available in or planned for English. Is it too much to hope one might soon be embarked upon?

Last autumn in the wake of the Farrera experience two attractively produced companion volumes of *en face* translations were published under the aegis of the Institució de les Lletres Catalanes. One is shared by Anna Crowe and myself. In the other and extending horizons further are two Hebrew poets Tamir Greenberg and Ronny Someck who at the formal launch told this traditional tale – take it how you will . . .

One day a Mouse found itself being chased by a Cat. Terrified, it managed to reach its hole and hide inside. For ages it cowered there, listening to the terrible miaowing. Eventually there was silence. Then came the sound of a Dog barking. I'm saved, thought the Mouse, my enemy must have been frightened away. So it came out. Only to find the Cat crouching over it. The Mouse looked up appalled and asked how the Cat, after all that barking, could still be there. Ah, replied the Cat, to survive nowadays you really must have two languages.

AFTER FARRERA

i for Anna Crowe

On the flight out
stewardesses feign
largesse: amidst
an alcoholic haze
I make mine a coffee
and slowly savour
the crisp bouquet
of your poetry,
its graceful filigree
the heart's tracery,
reassurance that
not even these days,
is refinement
wholly a lost art.

Once there you bloom
in the balmy air, warm
as a Scottish summer;
on a walk to the chapel
eagerly point out
'robins' pin-cushions'
among gleaming rosehips.
Later amidst Pisan
towers of dictionaries
your work, rendered
caringly into Catalan,
not merely bears
fruit but puts down
roots for the future.

ii for Francesc Parserisas

He brought us to no
mere castles in the air
but a mediaeval village
perched on a rock-face,
an icy Andorran skyline,
new sounds and meanings;

and with no clash
of temperament,
a troupe of skilled
translators bivouacking
on thrumming word-peaks
prior to the final ascent.

Or think of dowsers
tracking the source,
then the satisfaction
of transforming
one set of cascading
cadences to another.

As in a spring thaw
pure drops passed
caressingly, hand
to cupped hand,
their glistening flow
its own nourishment.

Barcelona Fantasies

Late one June afternoon in 1926 an elderly man in a black suit was going to pray – as he did daily – in Barcelona's St Philipp Neri Church. His appearance was shabby and down-at-heel: it's said he so disliked new shoes he had his brother wear them in for him. Crossing the Gran Via, probably deep in thought, he was hit and dragged along the street by a tram. No taxi-driver would take him to hospital. Passers-by tended him, until an ambulance came.

With no identification and nothing in his pockets he arrived unconscious at Sant Creu and was put in the public ward. The next day his friends, tracking him down, tried to have him moved to a private clinic. He insisted (it is said) that they let him stay where he was, 'among the poor'. Five days later, at the age of 74, the renowned architect Antoni Gaudí i Cornet was laid to rest in the crypt of the Sagrada Familia, on which he'd begun work half a century before. Ten thousand people followed his coffin.

In 1928 (the year Charles Rennie Mackintosh died) the foundation walls for the western façade of this 'Holy Church of the Atonement' were laid; and the 50th anniversary of Gaudí's death saw the completion of its astonishing spires. At first sight I found the building, still unfinished, fantastical; the four bell-towers of the eastern façade like a great mitre, darkening and lightening with the passage of the clouds. The words

Hosanna and *Sanctus* twine, and the bosses crowning the Apostle towers glint. Elsewhere figures seem to emerge from a coalescing mass of stone. An overhead fretwork of cranes seems integral to the structure.

Marvel though I did at the tapering spires, something about the continued building and a clash of styles in the later statues disconcerted me. So did the thought of the soaring cost, although to widespread and understandable relief this is borne not by the public but through donations: a significant proportion from those Japanese who have adopted Gaudí. I suppose my Presbyterian sensibilities were also offended by our having paid 800 pesetas each to step inside the railings – for a view really no better than from the street. I felt more at ease in the shade nearby, watching a Catalan *concours de pétanque* for free.

To the east we could make out through the trees a house-frontage with balconies and people on them. As we approached, they seemed more and more stilted and larger than life. We gasped at what was in fact a marvellous *trompe l'oeil*: each storey painted. Among the figures, Picasso and Miró. On entering the Cathedral of Santa Eulàlia you pass through an entrancing cloister with magnolias and a frog-fountain and come to the sacristy with an alabaster image of the Madonna. Finding the stygian chapels with their pyramids of candles and gilt carvings stifling, I sympathised with Hans Christian Anderson: 'The brooding half-darkness made denser by the incense and too oppressive for thoughts of God, I longed for the open courtyard, whose ceiling is the sky.'

What a joy we found, by contrast, the soaring interior of Santa Maria del Mar, its basilican solemnity heightened by plain octagonal columns spaced as widely as in any Gothic church in Europe. Its simplicity was no doubt largely due to its being stripped of its excrescences during the Civil War. Light fills the interior, reflects on polished stone. A wedding was in progress. Lengthy advice to the young couple, and pauses for flash-photos, allowed us to absorb the dignity and peacefulness of the building.

We kept, though, being drawn compulsively back to Gaudí: the secular Gaudí. Initially to his apartment blocks, which had a vigour I couldn't have imagined. The spartan Casa Calvet's tiles and balcony-rails are in tune with the buildings on either side. At the Palau Güell just off the Ramblas, wrought-iron grilles lead to the stables, two heavy oak doors to the coach-house. As with Mackintosh, slatted light-sources stunningly suggest through-space. Here too there was total harmony of design, down to the metal-work. Gaudí's chairs, though, looked much more comfortable.

The Casa Milá on its corner site is much more elaborate. Its billowing façade and undulating balconies are a cross between a cliff-face, a lived-in sculpture and something from a child's imagination. One moment you think of cave-mouths in rippling waves of sand; the next of stacked honeycombs. Yet precise draughtsmanship and engineering skills underpin every ridge and overhang. One column, like an elephant's foot, juts out across the pavement.

The attics, their brick vaulting a warm ochre, are exquisitely laid out and lit, as a museum. Twine models of arches, weighted to test that they would take the strain, hang like chandeliers over circular mirrors which show how the spires look, right-way-up. On the roof are chimneys and ventilators disguised as toad-stools, or sinister sentinels gazing through visors. We looked down at the inner courtyards, amazed at Gaudí contemplating (though not eventually incorporating) car-ramps and underground parking-bays.

Not even this prepared us for Güell Park, first meant as a garden suburb. The main gates are flanked by pavilions like something out of Hansel and Gretel, one also an elephant with trunk and howdah. There is a visual reminder (an axe-head motif) of the work-ethic; and the colours and symbols reflect Gaudí's intense Catalan loyalty and his Masonic links. Straight ahead the main staircase with its brilliantly coloured majolica salamander leads to an great open hall, its pillars slanting inwards to take the weight. Here a flautist was playing Mozart, his tone so mellow we stood to listen, then bought his CD.

Different sections of the Park are linked by tree-lined avenues. On one we passed an athletic young man who called out that my wife had bird-droppings on her bag and jacket. He offered a pack of tissues, pointing out that I was covered too. As she was taking off her bag a grave señor passing down the walkway behind the boy gravely shook his head and made warning signs, before moving on. Suspicious, we said we could manage. The boy went. The stains were wet mud. As we rubbed the bag clean two policemen arrived to check that we hadn't been robbed, and asking what the boy looked like.

We headed for a sandy arena bounded by a snake of balcony-seats in dazzling mosaic-work. In the shade we were serenaded by a guitarist dressed as a troubadour who then joined three figures in colourful costumes and animal heads, in a traditional dance. Nearby was our grave señor. We thanked him. As we left, he and his pals on adjacent benches were chortling at how but for him, we'd have fallen for one of the oldest tricks in the business.

Back on the broad Passeig de Gracia we sat at a café table to write postcards; our bags beside us, surely safe from threat. Directly across from us was Gaudí's Casa Batllo, with its balconies like half-masks. As we studied its mosaic-work through binoculars a trio of chattering gypsy-girls appeared, holding up sheets of cardboard with writing on them. One screeched at me, and assuming she was begging, I fended her off. Only then did I realise my wife was hanging on grimly to the handles of our bags as the other two clawed fiercely at them, then suddenly let go and fled. At the adjoining tables not a muscle twitched.

The image lingers. So does that of a boy still in short trousers, on a bench near the Mercat de St Antoni. I passed him on three different days. Each time he was in the same posture, passing a string of beads feverishly between his fingers, unaware of those milling by. His features could have been by Goya.

Most memorable though, was the architecture. The designs for Scotland's embryonic Assembly Building being then controversially in the hands of the Catalan Enric Miralles, we asked about him. Those we spoke to seemed to have heard of nothing he'd designed beyond a pergola and the archery range for the 1992 Olympics, and the cemetery at Igualada, a small town 25 miles from Barcelona (where the following year, at the early age of 45, he would himself be buried).

Miralles's assertion that his designs (more correctly, his concepts) are not the finished article, but leave leeway for subsequent inspiration and future development, is true to the tradition of Gaudí, the great improvisor. Coming ever closer to Nature, Gaudí saw as his model 'an upright tree; it bears its branches and these, in turn, its twigs, and these, in turn, the leaves . . . every individual part growing harmoniously, magnificently'.

One remarkable facet of Gaudí's genius is how his buildings fitted in: a flowering, in fertile soil. There was good reason for this. The second half of last century saw Barcelona expand. The Eixample (Extension) was planned, as Edinburgh's New Town and others had been, on a rectilinear grid, houses intended primarily for the moneyed upper-class. Height was restricted, light and air were to be let in. Two gracious boulevards, the Avinguda de la Diagonal and the Avinguda de la Meridiana, dissected the area.

All this coincided with the rise of *modernisme*, the Catalan version of art nouveau. But while Gaudí flourished daringly in its climate by claiming 'The straight line belongs to Man, the curve belongs to God', he can be even less circumscribed or conveniently categorised by it than Mackintosh, who was governed by the straight line rather than any pre-raphaelite swoon. Doggedly individualist, Gaudí also had strong Moorish and Gothic influences. Beyond that, the fluidity that was the hallmark of his buildings – as in the ripples of the Casa Milà – was integral to their structure, never a stylistic indulgence or concession to fashion. Similarly his seeming fantasies were not merely decorative but had deep seriousness and symbolic significance. In scale of output and reputation the two men could scarcely differ more.

Gaudí may have been mocked by cartoonists, and his Casa Milà nicknamed La Pedrera ('the stone quarry'). But he had his wealthy patrons – specially Count Güell. Further comparisons might have arisen, had Mackintosh's design for Liverpool cathedral not been rejected. As it was he sadly left Scotland in 1913, then moved to Port Vendres in the south of France and abandoning architecture, took up a new career as a painter.

These thoughts flitted through my mind on our last evening before a concert in the Palau de la Música Catalana. Hemmed in by the cramped streets of the Old City, Lluis Domènech i Montaner's glory of *modernisme* opened in 1908. Built into its ravishing exterior are busts of Bach, Beethoven, Palestrina and Wagner. Under a welter of arches and up a double-stairway, you come to a profusion of mirrors, mosaics, friezes, and coloured glass. It is like being inside a jewel cabinet. The 'spirits of music', maidens with different instruments, in mediaeval costume and linked with garlands, grace the curved wall with its broken tiles (*trencadis*). In dramatic contrast the proscenium arch, of soft white pumice, has a ghostly grandeur. Framing it in flowing stucco-work are columns releasing on one side galloping Valküre on winged steeds, and on the other a tangled tree of life.

Sensing little need to pit Mackintosh and Gaudí against each other, I settled to marvel at them for what they were: one a slender-stemmed glass of pure water, the other a beaker brimful of the exotic south. Then forgot both as the lights dimmed and the Barcelona Symphony Orchestra took over. The evening ended with Stravisky's 'Petrushka Suite': a perfect dying fall.

Back home we unpacked, and I remembered our mellow flautist. Wine poured, I put on his CD and we sat back anticipating Mozart. It turned out to contain a series of 'improvisations on guitar, flute and cello'. At first we thought the speakers were on the blink. But no: this 'music' comprised lengthy silences broken by sporadic plunks and squeaks. These persisted, disjointedly, track after track: not so much bird-noises . . . more aural blobs of mud. Punctuated by increasingly lengthy pauses.

Are they, I wonder, part of a sophisticated confidence-trick? Or a springboard to some art-form of the future? In an interview in *La Vanguardia* the day we flew back, a film-music composer Zbigniew Preisner was quoted as saying: *'Mi mùsica favorita es el silencio . . . El silencio es maravilloso, no?'*